LE-JOG-ED

LE-JOG-ed

A mid-lifer's trek from Land's
End to John O'Groats

Robin Richards
10/03/14

Robin Richards

Matador
9 Priory Business Park,
Wistow Road, Kibworth Beauchamp,
Leicestershire. LE8 0RX
Tel: (+44) 116 279 2299
Fax: (+44) 116 279 2277
Email: books@troubador.co.uk
Web: www.troubador.co.uk/matador

ISBN 9781783060535

British Library Cataloguing in Publication Data.
A catalogue record for this book is available from the British Library.

Typeset by Troubador Publishing Ltd, Leicester, UK

Matador is an imprint of Troubador Publishing Ltd

Printed and bound in the UK by TJ International, Padstow, Cornwall

To the memory of my parents:
Joyce & Ken Richards
who first introduced me to the hills.

Thanks

LE-JOG may be the walk across an island but, as I'm sure John Donne would have said, no LE-JOG-er is an island, so grateful thanks to Sarah – for everything, my family for their support, Wendy for proofreading and finally to my merry band of followers and supporters who LE-JOG-ed with me in spirit from End to End.

Taking Liberties

I have taken pains to ensure the account of my LE-JOG is as accurate as possible. At times however it has been necessary to change minor details such as names and locations in order to avoid embarrassment, libel lawyers and, quite possibly, lynch mobs.

John O'Groats

Inverness

Fort William

Milngavie
Edinburgh

Kelso

Edale

Birmingham

Bath

Barnstaple

Land's End

PART ONE – GO WEST OLD MAN

The Axe Man Cometh

We burst in through the doors of The Coffee Republic, a rabble calling out for cappuccinos, americanos and espressos. Some of our crowd ordered slabs of cake or biscuits to go with their coffee. I had no stomach for food. The sudden influx of a gaggle of lecturers quickly drove out the handful of late afternoon students eking out cups of cold coffee and generally avoiding classes.

We formed up into groups, scraping back tubular aluminium chairs and clustering around the smeared tables, each grouping according to their own specialism. This was no time for integration. The general nurse lecturers, by far the biggest group, quickly staked their claim to the centre of the room, pushing the children's nurses, the midwives and the learning disability nurses out to the fringes. That just left my own group, the psychiatric nursing lecturers, who, in keeping with their role as pariahs of the nursing profession, had to scrabble for the few remaining chairs and settle for being banished to the cold margins of the room, out where the doors opened into the kitchens.

Given the gravity of the situation there was a surprising amount of bright chatter and brittle laughter. Jokes were being told. The sort of jokes French aristocrats might have told each other in the tumbrils on their way to the guillotine.

It all felt a bit unreal to me, as if it was not really happening, more like taking part in a play. A play which

1

was badly scripted, where you only had a bit part, and no idea of the ending. The only thing you were sure of was that it was going to be a tragedy, not a comedy. All I knew was that there were countless people who had found themselves in a similar position to me, and some had been there more than once. I'd often wondered what it would feel like if it happened to me. How I would feel? How would I react? What I would say? What I would do? I still wasn't sure about the answers to those questions.

Of course none of this was a surprise. We'd all seen it coming months before. There was something in the way the senior staff and heads of departments had started behaving. There were just too many smiles and a forced cheeriness, a bonhomie that had never been there before, not even at the best of times. Whenever you met them in a corridor or at a meeting they would smile and tell you how everything was, 'Fine! Just fine!' We weren't fooled. We'd worked it out a long time before.

Ever since the job of teaching student nurses moved out of NHS hospitals and into universities we had held the contract for nurse education in our region. For preparing them, grooming them, and seeing them through the peaks and troughs and all the other alchemy necessary to transform the dowdy cygnet of a student nurse into the dazzling swan of a staff nurse who was fit to be let loose on an unsuspecting public. As our students were successful (most of them anyway), in that they passed their exams and the patients generally survived their tender ministrations, when the training contract came up for its periodic review it had always been renewed as a matter of routine.

But times had changed, or so we were told. There were new policies now, new ideas, new procedures, new competitors, there were sharks out there, and other less savoury predators. These new education providers would not be satisfied with just a slice of the action, they wanted the whole damn cake. Deadlines were set for renewing the contract. They came and went. There were temporary extensions, vague excuses and there was talk of putting the whole thing out to tender.

Coffee finished, we filed into a poorly-lit lecture theatre. On the stage below were our senior managers, glum-faced and sitting hunched like as many wise monkeys; speaking, hearing and seeing no evil. Especially seeing; it was a masterclass in avoiding eye contact. When everyone was settled they were joined on the stage by a man we had never met before. He was introduced to us as being from 'the centre of the university'. Matters had clearly slipped beyond our managers' control and they had been reduced to playing bit parts, demoted from chief mourners to the Greek chorus.

The man from 'the centre of the university' looked like a social worker who had been stuck in a time warp since the 1970s. His tweed jacket, with its brown leather elbow patches, was shapeless and fitted badly, his woollen tie was carelessly knotted and his cavalry twill trousers sagged where years of sitting had formed pockets for his knees. It felt like a bit of a let down. If someone is going to tell you that your job is going down the chute it would be nice to think that they first took the trouble to look in the mirror and run a comb through their hair. Instead we had a scarecrow who squinted through his pebble glasses and mumbled into his beard.

At least he came to the point quickly. The contract to train student nurses, he told us, had now been awarded to our rival university at the other side of the city. The next intake of student nurses would be our last and after that our operations would be progressively scaled down as our student numbers reduced and the department closed.

'And then what?' said a voice from the back of the room.

He hadn't invited questions and it clearly irritated him but he decided to answer anyway.

'Nurse training in this region will be the exclusive preserve of our rivals.'

'And what happens to our jobs?' said someone else.

'Everyone's job will be examined. For those who work primarily in first level nurse training, systems will be implemented to permit them, under certain conditions, to transfer universities.'

'What about the ones who don't work in first level nurse training?' said another voice from the back.

'Or the ones that don't meet those "certain conditions"?' said another.

'And what about support staff?' said someone else.

'Yes and the secretaries.'

'Let me make it quite clear.' He was struggling to make himself heard. 'We will attempt to absorb or transfer as many staff as possible.'

'Will anyone be left over?'

'Well we can't at this early stage …'

'What's going to happen to them?'

'Inevitably,' he said, raising his voice and pushing his glasses up his nose. 'Inevitably, there will be some staff we are unable to relocate.'

'You mean there will be redundancies then?'

'It's too early to say.'

'Compulsory redundancies?'

'Probably.'

'How probably?'

'Very probably.' The Axe Man had spoken.

That was the moment when the world, for me, slipped off its axis and stopped spinning. Well, for a bit anyway.

Common sense may have told me that I knew it was coming but that didn't lessen the impact as the bolt struck home. The gabble of the voices around me, the questions being shouted out, the bland, evasive replies from the stage, suddenly became distant and muffled, as if they were coming from the end of a very long and echoing tunnel. So this is what it felt like. This is what *they* felt like, those thousands of workers who, over the years, had filed into similar drab meeting rooms to be told by a faceless company hatchet man that their job, their pride, their livelihood and, lets face it for many of them, their sole reason for being on the planet, was soon to be no more.

The voices carried on around me. More questions, all of them seeking some reassurance, where no reassurances could be given. Some of my colleagues (my soon to be ex-colleagues) were downcast, some red-faced and angry. What about my job? What about my students? What about the new curriculum? What about the job, this job? The job I trained for, the job I've laboured long and hard over? The job I've given thirty years of my life to?

When the questioners started to repeat themselves and when it was clear that nobody was going to be satisfied by such answers as he could give, the Axe Man brought the meeting to an abrupt close and before we had chance to draw breath we found ourselves outside in the street, faces pale and shocked under the street lights. We stood in small groups clustering together for mutual support, shell shocked, still trying to take in everything we had just heard. And then, one by one, we drifted off into the night, home to tell our wives, our partners and our families.

The day after our encounter with the Axe Man was much like any other day at work, except nobody did any work. We drank even more coffee than usual and did quite a bit of gazing blankly into space, and a lot of getting together in little groups and telling each other how we'd been expecting this for months. This state of shock and awe persisted until mid-morning when one of our colleagues, returning from a visit to one of the other sites, discovered an estate agent nailing up a 'For Sale' sign on the outside of our campus building. This was the point that even the most positive amongst us began to realise that perhaps we no longer had a job for life. Our managers did, somewhat later, have the grace to concede that trying to sell the building under us was perhaps just a little tactless and that maybe it would have been a good idea to tell us first.

Call it redundancy or early retirement (our managers preferred to call it early retirement in my case), either way I, and a lot of the mates I'd been working with for years, were 'down the road'. In hindsight I might have taken 'down the road' a tad too literally. I went down the road all right, lots of roads as it turned out. I went for a walk. The longest walk you can do in Britain, without doubling back on yourself, is LE-JOG, Land's End to John O'Groats. So on a misty, drizzly and frankly uninspiring morning I stepped off the bus at Land's End with my boots blacked and my rucksack packed. It was just day sixteen of my redundancy – sorry, my early retirement.

Ambushed

It might seem something of big jump from being made redundant to packing my rucksack and setting off to walk from Land's End to John O'Groats, and I suppose in many ways it was. This is the point where I should make a grand statement of how this had always been a burning ambition of mine, that ever since I was a youngster I knew that one day I would be destined to walk from Land's End to John

O'Groats. I would like to say that, but if I did, it would be a lie. Well perhaps not a whole big fat whopper of a lie, but a fib, a half-truth at the very least.

I had always been a hillwalker, ever since I was a kid. I was born the son of parents who were keen walkers. My most vivid memories from childhood are of being winkled out of bed early during the weekends and school holidays, and setting off as a family to go for a walk. My mum would be striding out ahead, my dad would be carrying an old canvas and leather rucksack with the sandwiches and a flask of tea packed inside, and my big sister Jane and I would be lagging behind, usually moaning that we were tired, hungry, thirsty or that we wanted a rest.

When I was ten or eleven we joined a proper walking club, The Good Companions Rambling Club in Sheffield, and they opened up a whole new world beyond the local walks we had been on up to that point. And so, every Sunday, irrespective of what the weather was doing, we, as a family, would go out walking in the Peak District with The Good Companions Rambling Club.

There were not many books written about walking in the late 1960s so when John Hillaby's *Journey Through Britain* was published in 1968, it became a 'must read' for ramblers everywhere, and I can remember a copy being passed around the rambling club. I wasn't a big reader back in those days and I tossed it aside after only reading a few pages because I was disgusted that John Hillaby chose to wear lightweight Italian walking shoes for his trek. This was a time when nobody believed that it was possible to survive, if you ventured more than a couple of hundred yards away from the tarmac, unless you were wearing boots of the stoutest leather construction with thick cleated soles like the treads on lorry tyres. Back then we would wear the sort of boots which wouldn't have looked out of place on an expedition to K2 for a gentle stroll down Lathkill Dale.

I must have read Hillaby all the way through at some point, probably when I first became a keen reader in my early teens, and I must have forgiven him the Italian walking pumps because as I got older the idea of copying him and walking the length of Great Britain crystallised into something of an adolescent pipe dream. But it went no further than that. I lodged it in the back of my mind along with all my other, typically blokey type pipe dreams, like playing lead guitar in a rock band, scoring the winning goal in the Cup Final or getting into Gillian Granger's knickers.

I left school and mucked around for several years doing all sorts of dead-end jobs before I took a notion to train to be a psychiatric nurse when I was twenty-two. After that I didn't get out walking as often as I used to and the dream of walking Land's End to John O'Groats receded, but (unlike scoring with the fair Miss Granger or in the Cup Final), it never quite went away. Whenever I was having a bad time, and for 'having a bad time' read when things were not going very well at work, I'd go home and spread out the maps on the living room carpet, and start to plan possible routes.

On the whole I didn't think I'd come out of this redundancy-cum-early-retirement business too badly. I had become increasingly disenchanted with the job as the years had gone by. Fed up with top-down management where procedures, regulation and targets were seen as something akin to the Holy Grail and an atmosphere where individual talent, flair or initiative was viewed with suspicion by the powers that be, and quickly stifled. My ambition and career aspirations had become casualties along the way, steamrollered under an unstoppable and all pervading form of corporate daftness.

Most of my colleagues, especially those who still had young families, transferred to the 'other' university as the job and the contract to train student nurses moved across the city. But I didn't, I stayed behind with a few of the other old lags. There were still two or three years' work left in the job, seeing our remaining students through to the end of their nurse training. Then, when that was finished and done with, we had to promise to leave the building in a quiet and orderly fashion, and remember to switch out the lights.

As the days and the months passed after our encounter with the Axe Man I found myself ruminating more and more on what I was going to do with my early retirement when the job came to an end. Work, for most men (and a lot of women as well), is tied up with their whole sense of identity, their sole reason for living in some cases. Take that work away and there is the nagging suspicion that there just might not be an awful lot left. So what was I going to do with my time? How would I fill that void? Retirement, or so I told myself, shouldn't mean the end to any kind of active engagement in the world at large. But what sort of active involvement, and which world at large? I was buggered if I knew. I couldn't be destined for the scrap heap, surely, or not yet anyway? Thirty years of nursing couldn't be just casually set aside. I'd have to find something useful to do, but what? Who would want me now, now I was over fifty? I'd already discounted the idea of finding a little job still in the nursing field. I knew some of my mates were talking about working a couple of night shifts in a nursing home but I didn't fancy that at all. And anyway, a 'little job', any 'little job', would feel like a step backwards. If the nursing profession had seen fit to put me out to grass then so be it. I would make a clean break, old Florrie Nightingale could go hang, I'd find something different to do … quite different … very different … but what?

I suppose it was inevitable then that at some point my old idea of walking End to End would reassert itself and that's just what happened. It ambushed me one evening when I wasn't expecting it. I was pottering about in the spare room, sorting through a pile of old books, when I came across my ancient and dog-eared copy of John Hillaby. I turned it over in my hands and something like the tingling of an electric shock ran through my fingers, up my arms and right through my whole body. I could do this now, I thought, just as soon as I've finished work. I could pack a rucksack and go off and follow old Hillaby. This thought was followed just a nanosecond later with the thought of just how ridiculous it would be for a not very fit, fifty-two-year-old, soon to be ex-nursing lecturer who hadn't done any serious walking for years to set out on a mad venture like that. I realised my palms were sweating and I was starting to get a choking sensation in my throat. I put Hillaby down carefully on top of the stack of books and dried the palms of my hands on the seat of my jeans. It was ridiculous, totally ridiculous. I'd be away for more than three months and that wouldn't be very fair on Sarah, my wife. And I'd never get anything like fit enough. And I wouldn't want to carry a massive rucksack all that way. And I wouldn't fancy having to camp. Then of course there was the killer question. The big one, the question which has torpedoed countless expeditions, shot them clean out of the water before they'd even got off the drawing board. Just how many pairs of underpants would you need to pack for a trip like that?

The whole thing was a crazy notion and deserved to be scrapped. Phew. It was a close shave though.

But ideas like that don't just go away and, like an itch I couldn't scratch, this one kept on nagging at me. I floated the idea with Sarah, and she agreed, in principle at least, to me going and said it would be good for me. And I found myself thinking, purely theoretically at that stage (or so I told myself), about ways that I could actually make it happen. In the end I came up with what, in hindsight, seemed the logical solution. To attempt to do the walk in one go would take at least three months and to go from almost zero to three months of marathon walking seemed not so much a recipe for disaster as an Egan Ronay cordon bleu three course meal recipe for disaster, so I decided I would break it up into logical sections of say two or three weeks walking at a time and do it in a series of consecutive stages.

I have to say that had I been younger I would have liked to have done the walk all in one go, and purists may scoff but doing the walk in bite-sized chunks made it possible for me and logistically a whole lot easier. Each leg of the walk was like planning a separate fortnight's walking holiday and it kept the weight I had to carry in my backpack down to a minimum. I drew up my own set of rules: I would start at Land's End and finish at John O'Groats, walking each section consecutively. I would walk all the way and not use any mechanical form of transport such as escalators in shopping malls or ferries across rivers and estuaries. And at the beginning and end of each section I would find a specific landmark which would serve as my finishing point for one leg and the starting point for the next. And so, with all of the details settled, I started clearing my desk in readiness for the magical day when I would walk out of work for the very last time.

Starting Blocks

It might have been the merry month of May but standing at Land's End and staring out into the mist and the drizzle, I could only just make out the Longships Lighthouse a mile offshore. But the shop was open and so was the café so I bought some postcards and sat in the café writing them then I dropped them into the official postbox, where they would be franked 'Land's End'. There could be no turning back now. I'd used up all the diversionary tactics I could think of and couldn't put the evil moment off any longer. I went out into the drizzle and found the famous signpost which told me that John O'Groats was some 874 miles distant. I had my photo taken, smiling and looking a whole lot more confident than I was feeling inside, and then I set off walking.

The path curved over the headland for Sennen Cove, the next bay along. I was trying very hard not to think about John O'Groats but at Land's End it's almost impossible not to. The two names have become inextricably linked: Land's End to John O'Groats, John O'Groats to Land's End. The signpost may have said it was 874 miles away but in the public's mind the two places are tied together. People have gone from Land's End to John O'Groats by every conceivable means: bikes, cars, roller skates, I even saw someone on a unicycle. And anyway, I knew the distance of 874 miles was something of an arbitrary figure. 874 miles had a lot more to do with crows flying than walkers walking. Taking highways, byways and avoiding motorways into consideration, the minimum distance was closer to 900 miles. The Billy Butlin End to End race walk in 1960 was 891 miles long. But I was planning a green route, avoiding roads whenever I could and trying to keep to tracks and footpaths, so I was expecting to have to walk something closer to 1,200 miles (it ended up being 1,270 miles) before I reached that windswept rocky headland which is the most north-easterly corner of mainland Britain.

The adrenalin-fuelled high of taking the first few steps of my End to End walk lasted for all of five minutes and then reality kicked in. Is this it? I found myself thinking. Just walking now and nothing else? Start walking and keep going for 1,200 miles? My steps faltered and I ground to a halt. When I looked back, I could still see the Land's End signpost. What on earth was I thinking of? Let's be honest, I thought to myself, it's just not possible. I might as well have said that I'm setting out to walk to Narnia, or to Shangri-La, or even Mordor. 'I'm just off to the "Cracks of Doom", love. I'm giving Frodo a hand with the Ring. Don't wait up.'

I'm not sure how long I stood there looking back. I didn't want to be the first person in the history of End to End walking who packed in before he'd even covered the first half mile but it was a moment of brutal clarity after all the hype and hubris of buying new kit, catching a train to the West Country and setting off. It was by far the blackest moment of the entire walk and time sort of telescoped. At the end of this little crisis I'd like to report how I felt a great surge of resolution or some noble sense of purpose which welled up inside of me but the truth is I just started to feel pretty stupid standing there like a lemon, so I promised myself a pint when I got to St Just, hitched up my rucksack and set off walking again.

Chasing D H Lawrence

Day two of the walk and despite the rain I was making good progress. The road was slightly uphill beyond Bojewyan. My pack was feeling heavy, too heavy in fact, and I found I was running through a mental list of the stuff I'd packed and trying to think of things I could do without. Stuff I could either dump or post home when I reached St Ives. During those first stages of the walk I abandoned all sorts of unnecessary gear, and a few of the necessary bits as well come to think of it, in assorted rubbish bins along the length of Cornwall.

Just below the crest of the hill some dilapidated farm buildings stood back from the road, outside of which a black, mean-eyed dog stood out in the rain and regarded me with open suspicion. An old man was working in front of the farm buildings, bent digging mud out of a blocked drainage ditch, and not making a very good job of it. He was ankle deep in dark peaty water which sloshed around his wellies. He would bend and scoop up a shovel full of mud and black water and then, with great care and precision, slop it in on top of a heap of sludge on the bank of the ditch, where most of it would then cascade back down in muddy rivulets and drain back into the ditch. When I came alongside he stopped his work, leaned on his shovel for a moment and studied me carefully as I walked up. Then he took his cap off and, with a grubby forefinger, scratched his bald head, leaving a black mark behind shaped a bit like a comma. Then he put his cap back on and said, 'You know, lad, if you keep going, there's an oxygen station half a mile up the lane.' Then he turned his back to me and started to excavate another shovelful of mud out of the ditch.

The effect was instantaneous, my chest started to tighten as if it was being gripped and squeezed between a pair of massive invisible hands. My legs suddenly became heavy and curiously reluctant to move, I felt my heart begin to pound and my breath came in short rasping gasps. In fact I never properly got my breath back for the rest of the morning. Not until I was able to take my rucksack off and sit down for a rest in the pub at Zennor.

I had two compelling reasons to make a short detour off my route to visit the village of Zennor. Three if you counted my temporarily knackered state after my encounter with the grim ditch digger of Bojewyan. First I wanted to do the touristy thing and look at the chair with a mermaid carved on the side in Zennor church. Then I wanted to go to the pub, the Tinners Arms. With its low ceiling, oak beams and log fire crackling in the hearth, it was everything you'd hope for in a country pub. But this was more than just a beer stop. I was on a mission, a mission of literary research. During the First World War DH Lawrence and his German wife, Frieda, had stayed at the Tinners Arms for a time before they moved into a cottage nearby at Higher Tregerthen. They had grand ambitions of establishing an artists' community in Cornwall but things didn't turn out very well for them. For one thing the locals didn't welcome these Bohemian incomers and, this being during the First World War, they were frankly suspicious of the Teutonic Frieda. Although the Lawrences may not have helped their cause very much; the local people reported hearing them singing German folk songs at the tops of their voices when they passed by their cottage in the evenings and, as thousands of English lads were dying in the trenches over in Ypres and Paschendale around this time, unsurprisingly it didn't go down very well. The locals accused the Lawrences of being spies and of shining lights out to sea from the clifftops to help German submarines. In the face of this hostility they fled Cornwall and never returned. 'The Nightmare' chapter of Lawrence's book *Kangaroo* is generally believed to be based on his brief time at Zennor.

I drank up my beer and went out of the pub but before I quit Zennor altogether I wanted to see Zennor Quoit. Quoits are Neolithic tombs which are dotted across Cornwall, but they can be surprisingly difficult to find. During the morning I'd missed finding Chun Quoit in the rain, so I didn't want to miss out on this one.

Cornwall is stiff with tourist signposts of one sort or another. There were signposts to B&Bs, signs to beaches, signs to beach huts and signs pointing out where you could buy yourself an ice cream. Even the South West Coast Path, which I was nominally supposed to be following, had lots of signs. Especially lots of signs in places where there was no danger of you going wrong, then when the track became rather more confused or iffy the signs tended to become distinctive by their absence. Every form of tourist attraction was well signposted but when it came to their quoits, the Cornish were surprisingly coy. So it was going to be down to a serious bit of map reading, an activity which has never really been my strong suit.

The footpath to Zennor Quoit was only marked on my map by a thin, broken grey line and I wasn't at all hopeful of finding it. There was no signpost by the side of the road yet the footpath was there, exactly as marked on the map. It proved to be a very narrow circuitous path which meandered out across the open moor. It was flooded in parts and in other places knee-deep in wet gorse, brambles and heather. In fact finding Zennor Quoit was like spending an afternoon wading through a field of soggy Brillo pads. When I eventually found it I'm not sure it was really worth the effort. I was soaked and scratched from the knees down by this time. The quoit stood isolated on a rain swept moor, and consisted of five big, grey, upright slabs which would once have supported a larger 'roof' slab. Sometime, a couple of millennia back, the roof slab had slipped off to one side leaving the quoit in a partly collapsed state.

On the way back to the road I tried to increase my lifetime tally of quoits from one to two by trying to find Sperris Quoit. But this one was not as clearly defined as Zennor Quoit and I couldn't work out what was quoit and what was the surrounding crags. Then the rain started again, and with some spite to it this time, so I pulled my hood up and headed back through the brambles and gorse to the road.

There seems to be something of a history of running literary figures out of town in this corner of Cornwall. Not content with just seeing D H Lawrence off, back in the mid 1960s, when John Hillaby passed through on his End to End walk, he was unceremoniously marched out of town by the local constabulary after they caught him camping behind some beach huts. Bearing these facts in mind, I kept pretty quiet about my 1995 article for the *Nursing Times* and my one and only published short story and so I made it out of St Ives unscathed.

On the Beach

I think it's important to mention at this stage in the proceedings that all this End to Ending business was not what you would really call a mid-life crisis. I can say that with some degree of certainty because I'd been through all that mid-life stuff ten or more years previously. I'd even go so far as to say I enjoyed it. I'd swapped my glasses for contact lenses, bought myself a red sports car and combed my hair over the balding bit. I might have enjoyed it even more if I'd gone the whole hog and found myself a trophy girlfriend half my age but as far as a mid-life crisis went it wasn't bad.

So if this wasn't a mid-life crisis, what was it? I think I'll have to settle for calling it a mid-retirement or redundancy crisis. Much as I might try to pin the blame on poor old John Hillaby, if I'm brutally honest with myself a lot of this End to End walk was about flying in the face of the accepted attitudes to redundancy and retirement (early or otherwise). It was a project to get me through those first few days, weeks and, as it turned out, years of retirement. To try and shake off all of those snide, yet insidious, comments about pipes, slippers and being put out to grass. Something to provide a degree of the structure and sense of purpose which had previously come from work. Pipe and slippers be damned, if you can walk End to End you can't be that old and knackered.

Perran Beach just looked so inviting, and I'd already had enough of the rollercoaster-like clifftop paths which were such a feature of the South West Coast Path. Every day would start with a hike to the top of the cliffs, where the path, instead of staying at this airy and elevated level, would immediately plunge back down again to sea level and then, a matter of a few yards further on, it would start another long and tedious climb all the way back to the top of the cliffs with not a thought for the legs of the post-mid-life End to Ender. One South West Coast Path enthusiast I met at Tintagel Youth Hostel gleefully informed me that if you were to add up all the uphill bits on the South West Coast Path it would be the equivalent of climbing to the top of Mount Everest.

Perran Beach, a flat expanse of smooth sand still damp from the last tide, stretched out across the bay and, some distance away, the headland of Ligger Point looked purple in the haze. Out to sea, almost at the edge of my vision, the waves were piddling and tiny and they sparkled in the May sunshine.

There can be no better, or more exhilarating, sensation than walking along a beach, over firm, hard sand, with the wind blowing through your hair. Cutting across Perran Beach would give me a chance to pick up the pace and catch up on my schedule a bit. Over that hard, flat, even surface my legs would simply eat up the miles, my boots would hardly leave an imprint and the fresh sea breeze would blow away that persistent head cold which had been dogging me for the last couple of days. Or so I thought. I'd scarcely gone 300 yards away from the seafront at Perranporth when I realised I'd got it wrong; very wrong. The sand was not hard, nor was it very smooth. The wind was brisk all right, but it had worked itself up to something like a half gale and it had swung around to the north so I was walking with it full in my face.

If I had been smart I would have done something about it there and then, admitted my mistake, turned around and quickly backtracked, pretended I needed more coffee and headed back to the Dolphin Café at Perranporth without looking the least bit shamefaced. Then I could have headed off along the official route of the South West Coastal Path, through the dunes, and avoided the beach altogether. I could already see a party of walkers up there on the path and it looked to me as if they were making good time. But I didn't. I was still held in thrall by my wind-in-your-hair, sea-spray-on-your-face type of beach fantasy. The surface was sure to improve, I told myself, all beaches are like this, always softer near the shore where they've been churned up by the bucket and spade brigade. Half a mile out and it still wouldn't have been too late to retreat. After a mile I had stopped kidding myself. This was all a big mistake.

The sand, instead of being smooth, was a mass of wavy ridges, a bit like a corrugated iron roof. Neither was it as firm or as hard as it looked. The first step was like walking on a ploughed field or across uneven cobble stones. It would hold firm at first, until the full weight of my boot was on it, then it would sort of implode, crumble and turn into the mushy consistency of Demerara sugar. In order to keep upright on these shifting sands my legs would splay out to the side in something like an ungainly sort of doggy paddle. I've never tried to ski uphill through powder snow with roller blades strapped to my feet but if I ever did, I'm pretty sure that would be how it would feel.

To add to my miseries, the wind, which was coming in gusty and uneven blasts, had dried out the top layer of sand and was blowing it in clouds along the surface of the beach just above ankle height. I was wearing cropped, rolled-up walking trousers and my lower legs, which were not used to being exposed to the light of day, were beginning to feel as if they were being shot blasted.

No matter how hard or how fast I tried to walk through these quagmire sands, the crags at Ligger Point never seemed to get any closer and, if anything, walking faster and harder only made my boots sink in deeper and my progress slower and even more laboured. My floundering course, when I looked back at my footprints, had become anything but direct and they showed just how far I'd drifted out into the bay, where those piddling little waves were now becoming serious breakers and rolling in uncomfortably close. Another ten minutes and I would be paddling. Ten minutes on top of that and I might be swimming. I tried to walk even quicker. The official coast path was now something like a mile away to my right and on top of a set of steep and unstable-looking sand dunes, so retreat in that direction did not seem to be much of an option.

My calves, unaccustomed to this sort of treatment, were protesting and my rucksack, which seemed to have become a stone or two heavier, only served to push me deeper and deeper into the sand. I hadn't built up much in the way of fitness by this stage of the walk and anyway, Cornwall wasn't supposed to be like this. Cornwall was supposed to be the easy bit. Quicksand had never even figured in my reckoning.

I began to worry about the cliffs, still some distance away at Ligger Point. Assuming I made it there before being washed out to sea, would there be a path out from the beach to the top of the crags? My map was somewhat ambiguous on this point. It was becoming a race, me versus the tide. The only race I had ever won in my life was an egg and spoon race at Greenhill Primary School when I was six. I wasn't hopeful.

After three miles of remorseless trudging I seemed to hit on a patch of firmer sand and at about the same time the oncoming tide seemed to check its advance and my situation changed from critical to merely serious.

Another quarter of an hour of footslogging and I finally reached the base of the cliffs, where I found a nice broad path and a helpful signpost pointing to the top of the cliffs. I arrived hot, grimy and lathered in sweat, looking more like the survivor from a disaster movie than an End to Ender and feeling just a tiny bit foolish while all around me relaxed-looking holidaymakers were eating their sandwiches or building sandcastles on the beach.

On the map the route from St Agnes to Newquay via Perran Beach didn't look very far but with the up and down nature of the path, the convoluted coastline, the trauma of the sands and my energy-sapping cold I was at something of a low ebb. Then I committed a bit of a social gaff when I offended a small group of middle-aged ladies, sitting down taking afternoon tea outside the Bowgle Inn at West Pentire. I sat down at the next table and took my sock off revealing a blister so big it looked as if I was trying to grow another toe. But a night's sleep at Newquay ironed out a few of the creases and, with my blister lanced and surgically dressed, my End to End odyssey was once more a going concern. I'd promised myself an easier and shorter walk than the previous day, a modest six miles to Bedruthan Steps, and a more suitable distance for someone in my fragile condition.

But before I set off I had a few domestic jobs to attend to. A visit to the chemist's shop to stock up on patent medicines, blister patches and to buy a man-sized box of tissues (which only lasted until the next downpour before they were reduced to a soggy mass). Then I needed to do something about the weight of my pack so I made up a parcel of the sort of things I thought I might be able to manage without. I threw out some of my spare clothes and my nearly-thirty-years-out-of-date Land's End map. Thankfully when I'd reached St Agnes I'd walked onto my second map, which was new, accurate and up to date. Before I'd set out on the walk I'd thought that as I was going to be on my own I'd have lots of time in the evenings to read, so I'd packed a novel. Not even a light, short, holiday read type novel, but a weighty and mind-improving Penguin Classic. So with a silent apology to Anthony Trollope, *Barchester Towers* also went into the parcel to be posted home. For the rest of the walk my reading matter was restricted to whatever I could find in the bedside lockers of small hotels and B&Bs. I became an expert on tourist brochures, the Gideon Bible and glossy 'county' magazines from circa 1995.

The Hole-in-the-Wall

In a Gent's toilets outside Tintagel, there was a man trying to wash his hair. I had the impression that he must have been sleeping rough or camping somewhere nearby. For one thing he seemed to have an awful lot of gear: a rucksack, a kit bag and two plastic Tesco carrier bags full of groceries, all of which he piled in a heap against the wall opposite the urinals. Then he made a start on his ablutions. He took his shirt off to reveal a pale lardy torso with a beer gut and man boobs. On top he had a bullet-shaped head with no neck to speak of, and around his ample middle he had strapped a black bumbag, which presumably held his valuables.

It was the kind of public loo where the authorities had removed all the sinks and replaced them with vandal-proof, stainless steel 'hole-in-the-wall' hand washers. The kind where you stick your hands into a roughly round-shaped hole and press, first a button which sends down a squirt of soap, then another button which releases a trickle of tepid water and finally a third button which blasts hot air to dry your hands. By turning his head sideways he could just manage to get it into the hole. I watched the procedure with fascination, convinced that at any minute he would get his head stuck and I'd have to dash outside to phone for the fire brigade to come and release him. With his head inside he pressed the button marked water to wet his hair. When the water stopped running he carefully removed his head from the hole and, with his hair now dripping water across the floor, he went over to his mound of belongings and rummaged around until he found a bottle of herbal shampoo. He lathered up his hair then squeezed his head back into the hole-in-the-wall and pressed the water button again for a final rinse. It was a tight fit but he managed it, and his head came out with both ears still attached.

Outside it was a blustery morning with a cold wind whipping the sea up into whitecaps and there was a hint of rain in the air. Holidaymakers were battling against the wind and had wrapped themselves up against the elements in jumpers and cagoules. Seaside holidays were always like this when I was a kid. I was born and brought up in Sheffield and every summer we would take our holidays on the Yorkshire Coast, mostly at Bridlington. When we arrived there was always a gale blowing and clouds of spray being flung onto the promenade from a grey North Sea. When the weather let up a bit we would go down to the beach and sit huddled behind a candy-stripped canvas windbreak wearing our anoraks and woolly hats. We'd have hot tea out of a flask and I can still remember the grating feeling between my teeth as bits of windblown sand found their way inside the cheese sandwiches.

On the train to Bridlington I'd have read my copy of the *Beano Summer Special*. Splashed across the cover was always a picture of Biffo the Bear having a fun time on his holidays. He would be on the beach wearing a pair of swimming trunks and building sandcastles, or he would be dipping a shrimping net into the rock pools while crabs nipped at his toes, and all the time the sun shone down from a cloudless sky. Not a woolly hat, an anorak or a windbreak in sight. Somehow I could never quite square up Biffo's holidays with ours. It was my dad who finally sorted it out for me. 'I don't think,' he said, 'that Biffo the Bear ever took his holidays on the Yorkshire Coast.'

You don't have to be in Cornwall long to discover just how proud the Cornish are of their very Cornishness. Beside a Cornishman even a Yorkshire man's pride at being born in God's-Own-County seems to pale by comparison. Right across the county the flag of St Piran, a white cross on a black background, unofficially adopted as the Cornish flag, is everywhere, on cars, pubs and in windows.

As I worked my way through the county it came

across as a bit of a siege mindset. The words 'NO ENGLISH' were scratched on a National Trust sign at Trabarwith Strand. There was even a movement that Kernow (the Gallic name for Cornwall), should become an independent country. Every year they are invaded by armies of visitors and holidaymakers and an increasing number of incomers who buy second homes, which pushes up the price of properties to far beyond the reach of local home buyers. The village of Rock, across the River Camel from Padstow, has become the almost exclusive preserve of millionaires. As I made my footsore way into Newquay, past Fistral Beach, the Mecca for surfers, on the wall of a new development, roughly scrawled in black letters at least two foot high, were the words 'LOCALS ONLY'.

At Watergate Bay I stopped at the beach café for elevenses. I had quickly developed a great affection for these beach cafés. Every cove and inlet in Cornwall has one and they were heaven-sent for the End to Ender. Some were quite modest affairs, just a beach hut, selling tea in Styrofoam cups, ice creams and lumps of stodgy fruit cake wrapped in cling film. And some were smart establishments with indoor seating, selling freshly-brewed coffee and homemade cakes and pasties. So much for thinking I'd shed a few pounds on my walk.

'Why is it,' said Tilda, 'everybody thinks I'm walking the wrong way on the South West Coast Path?' She had a point. If you said you were walking the South West Coast Path, everyone you met, in the shops, the B&Bs and youth hostels, assumed that you had started at Minehead and would be working your way west towards Land's End. What's more, all the guidebooks seem to expect this too and they were all written with that in mind, which made trying to follow them and, in effect, reading the route back to front, a bit of a puzzle for such as Tilda and me because we were both going in the 'wrong' direction. This didn't bother me half as much as it did Tilda because, with her massive pack, bright orange waterproof and boyishly-cut blonde hair, she was a bit of a stickler for efficiency.

I didn't worry about working back to front in the guidebook. In fact by the time I'd reached Tintagel, which was where I first met Tilda, in the common room of the youth hostel there, I'd already given up on the guidebook and mine had been posted home along with all the other gear I'd found surplus to requirements.

'I hate it when I get lost,' said Tilda. 'And when it is the guidebook's fault I become furious.'

I'd gone adrift again only that morning. It certainly hadn't been the guidebook's fault, or the map's fault for that matter, although I did tell myself that if it hadn't been raining quite so hard, and if I'd been looking at the map a bit more often, I would have headed down the lane where I should have gone instead of wandering into the farmyard.

'Are you lost?' said the farmer.

'I don't know, am I?'

'Aye, lad, I think you are.'

Tilda was the only other End to Ender I'd met so far. She was still a year or two short of her thirtieth birthday yet she was a veteran long distance walker and had completed routes all over Europe. She had taken leave from her job as a freelance interpreter in Holland to walk End to End and had planned her route meticulously. First, she told me, she would go the wrong way along the South West Coast Path, and then she was going to work her way up the west side of the country, along Offa's Dyke, dipping into Wales, then take in the Lake District before crossing the border into Scotland and going up through the Highlands all the way to John O'Groats.

Unlike Tilda I was not sticking too closely to the South West Coast Path, which tracks around every headland and into every cove. I would frequently swerve off-route and cut inland, especially when the official route made long detours out onto promontories and peninsulas like the one at Hartland Point. Cutting down some of the Cornish back lanes saved me miles, and sometimes days, of walking. Even if it did mean a bit of roadwalking, the Cornish lanes in the spring didn't have very much traffic to trouble me and the hedgerows were a mass of wild flowers. The walls, which edged both sides of the lanes, were constructed from layers of stone and turf sandwiched together. Over the years they had become overgrown so the stone was almost completely hidden. They were like mini nature reserves, steep narrow banks of grasses, weeds and flowers sheltering voles, stoats and nesting birds. I'd even seen rabbits hopping along the flattened tops of the walls, using them as their own private highway.

Tilda was the only person I'd met on the walk so far that I'd owned up to and admitted that I was in fact walking Land's End to John O'Groats. This was not because I was trying to be modest or didn't want to be part of some sort of End to Enders community, but because saying too much about it, that early in the walk, felt a bit too much like tempting fate. There were still an awful lot of miles to cover and a lot which could go wrong. At first I would just tell the people I met that I was walking part of the South West Coast Path, and then later I'd just say I was walking whichever long distance path I happened to be on at the time. If I wasn't on a long distance path people tended not to ask anyway and I kept quiet about what I was up to. For a long time I kept my true objective pretty quiet and it wasn't until I was a good bit north of Hadrian's Wall that I started to feel I could be a bit more open about my intentions and I'd own up and tell the people I met that my sights were ultimately set on John O'Groats.

Clovelly

On my grandmother's wall, when I was a child, there was a picture of Clovelly. A tiny circular picture, which couldn't have been more than four inches in diameter, set under a dome of pebble glass. Years of the sun shining through the window and onto her wall had faded it so there really wasn't much picture left to see. Just a washed-out blue background etched with scratchy black lines which showed a rather stoical-looking donkey, wearing basket panniers, standing halfway up an impossibly steep cobbled lane in-between two rows of rustic cottages. It was the sort of scene where you expected, at any minute, to see a young lad with a cloth cap on his head come freewheeling down the hill on a shopbike delivering Hovis. I loved this picture when I was a youngster and I always wanted to go there. I wanted to pet the donkey and I wanted to freewheel down the hill on my bike.

It had been raining heavily since early morning. I'd set off with Tilda from the youth hostel at Elmscott, but when she said she was going out to the headland at Hartland Point I decided to keep to a more inland course. In the mist and the rain I just didn't think Hartland would be worth the effort. It was the kind of day when there was nothing you could do but hunch your shoulders against the rain, pull your hood down over your eyes and slog on, while the cars swished past with their windscreen wipers going and gloomy-looking faces peering out through the misted windows.

At Brownsham I followed a sign for a bridleway. But it didn't say where it was a bridleway to, and I spent most of the afternoon slithering around on muddy paths through dripping woodland, never totally lost, but never sure quite where I was. I passed a farm at one point where a beagle hound, with a forlorn look on his face, looked bleakly out of his kennel at me. His expression seemed to say, 'On a normal day, I'd do my job. I'd rush out barking and I'd see you off. But today, well, today it's just too wet to bother.'

The bridleway came out onto the clifftop not far from Clovelly and a quarter of a mile further on I found a small wooden shelter which was open at the front and had a bench seat inside. It was the first chance I'd had to get out of the rain all day. I'd been sitting there for ten minutes, just enjoying the sensation of not being rained on, when Tilda found me. Her orange cagoule was streaming water and the rain had frizzed the front of her blonde hair. She said it was too wet to camp so she was going to press on into Clovelly to see if they had internet access at the visitor centre, and then she was going to find a B&B.

When I finally reached the village I was soaked through, my rucksack was dripping and my map had been reduced to a sodden heap. I arrived at the top of 'The Street.' A steep cobbled lane leading down to the harbour where the donkey, in my grandmother's picture, had been so patiently standing. I was wrong about riding a shopbike down the hill. Such was the gradient that riding down on anything with wheels would be the next best thing to suicide. No wonder the locals still use wooden sleds to shift stuff up and down The Street. The donkeys were wisely keeping out of the rain that afternoon but there was plenty of evidence of their passing on the cobbles.

I was cold and I was wet. I hadn't eaten since breakfast and decided I would appreciate the period charm of Clovelly a whole lot more once I'd found something to eat and drink, preferably something warm, something cheerful and something filling. The cafés were all packed to the doors so I made my way between the old fishermen's cottages to one of the pubs. There was a warm fug in the bar and all the tables were taken by visitors escaping the rain and tucking into beer and pub meals. I pushed my way through the throng, reached the bar and asked to see the menu. The woman standing behind the bar gave me an appraising look from head to toe in the way that only pub landladies can. She took note of my muddy boots, my rucksack, my dripping waterproofs and then, in the fashion of landladies for centuries, she folded her arms and told me they had stopped serving food ten minutes ago. She suggested I went back out into the village and buy myself a pasty. But, once inside and out of the rain, I didn't much fancy going back outside into the wet so I settled for a pint of beer and a bag of cheese and onion crisps instead. The only place I could find to sit in the pub was on a three-legged stool at the end of one of the packed tables. All the other places were taken by remarkably dry-looking people who were all tucking into plates of bar food. Next to me there was a smartly-dressed young couple who were busily pushing chips into a fat and gurgling toddler.

I drank my beer, finished my crisps and went out into the rain again. I climbed back up The Street; at the top, just beyond the donkey sheds, was the visitor centre and inside the visitor centre there was a café. At last I was able to get something warm to eat and drink. After two mugs of coffee and a sandwich I was beginning to feel a bit more like a human being again. I'd even recovered enough to start to take an interest in my surroundings and so I decided to take a stroll around the visitor centre. All I wanted to do that afternoon was mooch around for a bit, look at whatever was on display, maybe buy a postcard or two, and generally kill a bit of time before I set out for Higher Clovelly and the B&B where I was planning to stay the night.

After a few minutes of studying the usual displays of period artefacts, rustic fishing gear and sepia photographs of the village back in the old days, I began to have the distinct feeling that I was being watched. I looked up from the display cabinet to discover that one of the attendants, an elderly woman with wild grey hair, fierce blue eyes and an illegible name badge pinned to her bosom, had planted herself squarely in front of me.

'Excuse me,' she said, fixing me with her gimlet-like eyes, 'but if you're going to the village, you've got to pay.'

I was a bit taken aback but I managed to stammer something to the effect of: 'Well I'm not going to the village but thank you for asking.' I didn't think it was any of her business that I'd already been.

'It's a private village and you've got to pay.' She had a venomous way of spitting out her words and I was glad I'd kept my waterproofs on.

'Good job I'm not going to the village then,' I said.

'Why would you come all the way to Clovelly,' she said, 'and not visit the village?' The other customers at the visitor centre were starting to look around by this point, to see what the commotion was about.

'Madam,' I replied. 'I am a middle-aged man who has very recently consumed a pint of beer in the pub and two large mugs of coffee in your café. There is only one place I am going to be visiting imminently, and I promise you it isn't going to be the village.'

And I walked away in what I hoped was a purposeful

manner, leaving a set of footprints across the floor. But she wasn't to be put off quite so easily and she pursued me across the visitor centre. Before I'd reached the next display of old sepia photos she was squaring up to me again. 'You are!' she spluttered. She was getting herself quite excited by now and her bosom, with its indecipherable name badge, was wobbling up and down. 'You're going to the village!' She threw an arm out, her index finger pointing towards what I suppose was the direction of the harbour. 'You are going to the village. You are going to the village now, *and you've got to pay!*'

I could see that only hard cash or my absence would appease her so, with as much dignity as I could muster, and a bladder close to bursting point, I turned on my heel and walked out of the visitor centre. I walked away from the village, away from The Street, away from its donkeys and away from its grey-haired guardian as fast as my muddy boot prints would take me. My demeanour may have been ruffled but at least my wallet remained intact.

I would like to say that I never went back or ever darkened their doors again but, when I discovered that my B&B didn't do evening meals, I realised that if I wanted to have anything to eat that night I would have to go back down to the village again. As it was, I waited until after dark before I skulked back. I gave the visitor centre a wide berth, expecting that at any minute the wild-eyed harridan and self-appointed keeper of Clovelly's Privy Purse would leap out and once again demand money with menaces. I did not, by the way, see one sign or any clue whatsoever to inform me that it was a private village and that you were expected to part with a substantial chunk of the readies for the privilege of treading its donkey-soiled cobbles.

Clovelly, in the evening after the visitors had gone, was a different place altogether. The Street was deserted, apart from a black cat doing his rounds, and even he came up and rubbed himself against my legs wanting a fuss. It felt a lot less like a tourist attraction or the set of a BBC costume drama and a lot more like a proper village. More like the village I'd seen all those years ago in my grandmother's faded picture. I went to a different pub this time, where the landlady was friendly and obliging. I watched the England football match on the TV there while I had a beer, and she served me up a very respectable steak and ale pie.

Tooled-up

There are footpaths, and then there are 'virtual' footpaths. This not very profound insight occurred to me as I pulled my foot out of a stinking mush of decomposing gloop for the umpteenth time that morning, and stopped to survey the damage. Brown, evil-smelling slime oozed down my leg and started to pool inside my boot.

Occasionally, and usually very unwisely, some latent sense of adventure would seize hold of me and I would take a notion to veer off the approved route and follow some quiet backlane or seldom-used footpath to either add a little variety to the proceedings, or to find what I thought would be a more direct route. These variations on a theme were seldom as successful on the ground as they looked on the map.

I'd encountered my first virtual footpath on the road between Copperhouse and Wheal Alfred, where the walled lane I was searching for suddenly morphed into a field of golden corn which was swaying gently in the breeze. I put that down to the map I was trying to navigate by; close inspection revealed it was almost thirty years out of date. But worse was to come, another virtual path between Portreath and St Agnes. That one came to an abrupt end at a barbed wire and chain-link fence which blocked the route with notices from the Ministry of Defence fixed to it, threatening me and everyone else with all manner of dire and official retribution if we didn't 'Keep Out'. Then I found another useful-looking path which would have avoided a particularly busy stretch of the A39 trunk road, but again it was a virtual path that clearly existed in some other time-space dimension where walkers venture at their peril. That one resulted in an unpleasant and unplanned hike along a main road choked with holiday traffic and a close encounter of a very real kind with a coal wagon, where I only avoided disaster by lying spread eagled against the bank while my whole life flashed before my eyes.

So I really should have known better by the time I reached Buck's Mills, a few miles east of Clovelly, and headed inland on a short path which I thought would save me a bit of roadwalking. It looked quite hopeful at the start and, unlike most virtual footpaths, this one had a signpost, a stile and it began with a clearly-defined track. After such a promising start things quickly started to unravel. It swerved away into a steep-sided wooded valley where it promptly gave up any pretence whatsoever of being a footpath. The woods became dark and the trees were packed tightly together. The valley became a sudden severe climb and rapidly narrowed into an overgrown ravine. The track underfoot turned wet and was choked with thick vegetation, the trees closed in from both sides and seemed to meet overhead and on the banks between the tree trunks thickets of lush green brambles and dog roses were growing armed with vicious spikes and thorns. I found I was wading uphill through soggy leaf mould and primeval gunk which must have been the accumulation of at least a couple of millennia. With every step I sank up to my knees in rotting goo. The brambles started to throw out long, creeper-like tendrils which hooked onto my skin, tugged at my clothes, snagged on my rucksack and, from time to time, cheekily snatched the hat clean off my head. In less than half a mile a pleasant woodland path had become a raging Amazonian rainforest; throw in an anaconda or two and a troop of howler monkeys and the transformation would have been complete. Retreat looked a less inviting prospect than going on. The brambles and creepers had closed in behind me, where they had knotted and tangled across the path. Like a Venus flytrap it had drawn me in but wouldn't let me go. I was becoming hot, panting for breath, and my shirt was sticking to my back. I felt as if I was slipping into the otherworldliness of the virtual footpath and at any minute I expected to see Indiana Jones come crashing downhill past me, being pursued by a massive stone ball.

After what seemed like an age of hacking through the undergrowth (but which I later found out, when I looked at the map, was actually a disappointingly short distance) the angle of the hillside began to ease, the jungle started to retreat, I retrieved my hat for one last time from the strand of bramble which had filched it and I emerged blinking and dazed out into the sun. The ravine became a path again, which in turn became a pleasant lane, which quickly led up to the A39 trunk road and back to the real world. I found myself standing on the edge of the road looking back the way I'd come. I was feeling a bit like one of Dr Who's ex-assistants who stand there with bemused looks on their faces just after the Tardis has departed and wonder if they have imagined the whole darned thing. All I had to show for my brush with the virtual space-time continuum was a shirt torn in half a dozen places and a similar number of scratches on my arms and legs which were just beginning to seep blood.

I crossed the main road near a place called Watershute and headed down a minor road, past a small cluster of buildings, my objective for the day being to reach Bideford, which was still some nine miles away. One of the buildings, a farmhouse, which looked particularly prosperous, was smart and newly painted. It stood well back from the road, almost hidden behind neatly-trimmed hedges. I had already walked past the gateway and, minding my own business, was still dusting myself down, rooting leaf mould out of my socks and picking bits of twig from out of my hair when a low-pitched growl from behind made the hairs on the back of my neck stand on end. The dogs, two of them, shot towards me like as many furry ground-to-earth missiles. They moved with the speed and grace of greyhounds newly released from the traps. Their feet hardly seemed to touch the ground as they sped forward, ears pressed flat against their heads, lips drawn back revealing yellowed fangs and gobbets of saliva, which had flecked their muzzles, flying off in their slipstream. The one in the lead was dark brown, with muscular shoulders, a broad head and green angry eyes. I don't know much about dogs but this one looked as if it might have been a cross between a mastiff and a grizzly bear. The second hound lagged behind, he was a washed out grey colour, older, smaller and a whole lot sneakier. He was a yappy sort of dog who made more noise but his heart didn't really seem to be in the whole enterprise. They were on me before I realised what was happening.

I'd been grateful several times that I'd brought a trekking pole along with me and on this occasion it was a lifesaver. I wasn't expecting to be set upon by raving beasts and it was only by chance that I still had the pole in my hand after the scramble up through the ravine. If I hadn't, my Land's End to John O'Groats odyssey would have come to a sudden and painful end right there and then, courtesy of their two sets of fangs. Grizzly screeched to a halt when I waved the pole in front of his nose, his massive paws leaving four skid marks across the tarmac. The old guy made a dummy to the right then made a lunge for my left ankle but I was backing away down the lane so rapidly he missed by a couple of inches. In addition to flailing around with my trekking pole I shouted a few choice words at these Hell hounds; I can't remember the exact words but I know I wouldn't care to repeat them in polite company. Their first attack foiled, they tried to outflank me with a pincer movement but gave that up when I took to whirling around, dervish-like, with my trekking pole extended out at arms length. From behind the hedge I heard a woman's voice bellow out, 'Come back in 'ere, you little bleeders.' A look of disappointment crossed Grizzly's face and after a baleful look in my direction they both started to slink off back towards the gate. The old guy looked relieved and a little bit breathless but Grizzly couldn't resist one more rush at me just when he thought I'd let my guard down. But for me that was a lunge too far and, seeing them in retreat, fear turned to anger and it was my turn to take a run at him. He quickly backed off with an affronted look on his face which seemed to say, 'Look, this isn't in the rules. I'm the dog, you're the man and it's me who is supposed to chase you'. He paused in the gateway to bare his yellow fangs at me one last time, then he went back behind the hedge to join his mate and wait for the next unsuspecting passer-by, hoping no doubt that they'd be a bit luckier next time and not choose a walker who'd had the good fortune to come along already tooled-up.

The Great Billy Butlin Walk
When it was certain that I was finishing work for good, the

first thing people would ask me was what I was going to do with myself and I'd tell them that I was going to walk from Land's End to John O'Groats. It prompted a mixture of reactions. Some people thought it was a great idea, some said they'd always wanted to do something similar and wished they could come with me. Some said I was mad, and several told me quite bluntly that I'd never make it. One cheerful soul told me they'd send me back home in a bucket and he was rewarded with guffaws of laughter all around from everyone else in the bar. I quickly crossed him off my postcard list. But it was some of the older folks, the people of my parents' generation, who came up with the oddest reaction. They would pause, gaze into the middle distance and a faraway look would come into their eyes as if they were searching for some lost or forgotten memory. Then something would seem to click in their heads, their eyes would start to sparkle and they'd nudge me in the ribs and say, 'Oh Land's End to John O'Groats! Oh aye, Billy Butlin eh?' And then they'd wander off smiling and chuckling to themselves and leaving me totally flummoxed. It took me weeks to fathom this one out.

The whole idea of walking from John O'Groats to Land's End was thrust into the public consciousness in January 1960 in the form of a short, fifty-six-year-old Russian émigré called Dr Barbara Moore. It is something of an understatement to say that Dr Moore was a woman with a mission. She was a radical vegetarian who set out to prove how superior a vegetarian diet was by making a series of increasingly long marathon walks while living on a diet of nuts, fruit juice and honey. Vegetarianism was still something of a rarity in the late fifties and early sixties and consequently she received a massive amount of press attention.

Her first long distance walk was from Birmingham to

Marble Arch, then in December 1959, she set out from Edinburgh and walked the 373 miles to London in just over seven days. A garage owner, Wilfred McDougall from Bilson in Staffordshire, offered a prize of £250 to anyone who could beat her time. James Holdsworth, a joiner from Bradford, set out to claim the prize but he gave up after only twenty-seven miles because the weather was bad. On the 5th January 1960 *The Times* reported that Mr T Haywood, a lorry driver from Birmingham, had beaten Barbara Moore's time and had claimed the £250 prize. The following day Dr Moore announced to the world that she was planning to walk 1,000 miles from John O'Groats to Land's End and that she would start the following week. She invited Mr Haywood to join her. He declined and said he needed a rest.

Dr Moore was not the first person to walk from John O'Groats to Land's End nor was she the first long distance walker. The Naylor brothers, Robert and John, completed an End to End at a fairly leisurely pace in 1871, stopping off to visit places of interest along the way. Arguably the greatest marathon walker was 'The Celebrated Captain Barclay' who, on Newmarket Heath, between June and July 1809, in what was hyped to be 'The Greatest Ever Sporting Event', walked 1,000 miles in 1,000 hours for 1,000 guineas. That is, he walked one mile every hour, day and night, for one thousand hours (a thousand hours is just over forty one and a half days). And after this feat of endurance Captain Barclay took only the briefest of rests. Eight days later he was fit enough to join his regiment and sail off to the wars against Napoleon.

Dr Moore set off from John O'Groats on 13th January 1960. Her progress was widely reported in the press as a quirky, eccentric story and welcome light relief amongst the usual gloomy January news. When she passed through

Wick the town's girls' pipe band turned out to escort her through the streets. On 14th January *The Times* reported she had covered almost fifty miles and reached Berriedale, where she was resting with 'a bad ankle'. Her ankle must have recovered quickly because she reached Land's End to great acclaim and media attention just twenty-three days after leaving John O'Groats. Walking End to End in twenty-three days in the depths of winter, for a fifty-six year old woman on a diet of nuts, fruit juice and honey has to be a good walk by anybody's standards. The newspapers were filled with admiration. She would go on to top even this feat in the summer of 1960 when she walked 3,387 miles from San Francisco to New York in eighty-five days.

One man reading the press reports of Dr Moore's walk with rather more than just a passing interest was the holiday camp entrepreneur Billy Butlin. He thought the matter over while he took his morning bath then called his executives together and announced that they were going to organise a 1,000 mile walk from John O'Groats to Land's End and they were going to start straight away.

Billy Butlin was a man who had shown the world that he could make things happen. He had been born in 1900 in South Africa, where his parents had emigrated shortly before. His paternal grandfather was a clergyman but his mother came from a long tradition of travelling show people and the young Billy was a showman through and through. When he was demobbed from the army after World War I he began work in travelling fairgrounds and amusement parks, eventually organising sideshows for Bertram Mill's Circus. In1936 he opened the first Butlin's holiday camp at Skegness and staffed it with his famous Redcoats. It was a huge success and soon he had opened a network of holiday camps across the UK. By 1947 he was a millionaire.

One of the foundations of Billy Butlin's success was his flair for publicity. He had organised the annual Cross Channel Swim since 1947 and later gained considerable media attention by saving Big Charlie – the largest elephant in captivity and veteran of the *Tarzan* movies – from being put down. Butlin successfully brought the elephant and his mahout to his camp at Filey, where they were a big attraction for years. The media sensation of Dr Moore's walk was heaven-sent for Billy Butlin as it focused attention on his holiday camps in the depths of winter, when nobody was really thinking about holidays.

At 5pm on Friday 26th February 1960, less than a month after Barbara Moore had completed her walk, twelve rockets were fired into the sky above John O'Groats to herald the mass start of the first and only Billy Butlin Walk. Had the walk been planned to start a week earlier it would never have happened because Caithness was under a heavy fall of snow and locked in the grip of icy weather. Billy Butlin arranged for snow ploughs to clear the roads and organised schools and church halls to be opened for rest stops and so the walk went ahead.

With prize money of £1,000 for the first man and £1,000 for the first woman the race was hugely popular and generated over 4,000 applications. In a letter to all competitors Butlin stressed how tough the walk would be, how local services would not be able to meet everyone's needs and that, in effect, it was up to them to be self-reliant. By the start the walkers had been whittled down to just over 700.

If the race was proving a big hit with the general public it was less popular with Scottish authorities. 'Outrageous!' thundered the Lord Provost of Glasgow to *The Times*. And he accused Billy Butlin of turning Dr Moore's walk into a mere advertising stunt. The Chief Constable of

Caithness tried to have the walk cancelled because of the bad weather and Sutherland County Council asked Mr Maclay, the Secretary of State for Scotland, to intervene but he replied that he had no powers to stop the race. So the Butlin race was scheduled to start as planned.

The Billy Butlin Race was 891 miles long, and not the 1,000 miles as often suggested. The early stages of the race through wintry conditions in the far north of Scotland, were especially gruelling despite the help and support of locals, who frequently took the walkers in, fed them, dried their clothes and gave them somewhere to sleep for the night. Amongst the ragbag army of walkers who converged on John O'Groats there was a fair smattering of eccentrics and no-hopers, many of whom dropped out of the race very early on. The bulk of the walkers, however, were quite well prepared and set out with hopes of winning the £1,000 prize, but they could not compete with the serious athletes who were fit, well organised, and had brought along pacemakers and backup teams. Sadly the fourth category of competitors were the cheats. Cheating became a problem from very early in the race. Some had arranged for cars to speed them ahead through sections of the walk, others caught buses or thumbed lifts in lorries and vans. To combat this threat to the competition Butlin had to arrange mobile checkpoints to try to catch them out.

The men's race was won by Jim Musgrave from Doncaster, who arrived at Land's End fifteen days, fourteen hours and thirty-one minutes after leaving John O'Groats. He was photographed by the famous Land's End signpost being presented with his cheque by Billy Butlin. The winner of the women's race was eighteen-year-old Wendy Lewis from Liverpool, who said she was going to use her winnings to open a hairdressing salon.

The events of that winter and the efforts of Dr Barbara

Moore, Billy Butlin and his weary band of gallant footsloggers served to lodge the idea of walking Land's End to John O'Groats in the public consciousness as the archetypal British endurance walk. For me, when I walked along the seafront, close to the end of the South West Coast Path, and I passed the curious tent-like structure of white peaks which was Butlin's holiday camp at Minehead, I couldn't help but stop and reflect that if it hadn't been for what Sir Billy and co. had started back in 1960, I might not have been standing there at that moment, in my boots, cagoule and rucksack. And, but for them, I might still be out there in my own personal wilderness, struggling to find a way of misspending my early retirement.

The Hindmarsh Principle
When I reached Barnstaple it marked the end of the first leg of my walk and the chance to go back home for a few weeks, wash my (by now) rather whiffy kit and generally have a bit of a breather before I was back there again in the late summer to pick up the walk from the exact point where I'd left off (I was really picky and anorak-ish about this).

I hoisted my backpack on to my shoulders and headed out of town along Bear Street but before I'd gone more than a couple of hundred metres the rain started and I had to stop and pull my waterproofs on. It was on and off rain all day. I steered an inland course, mostly along quiet backroads, past fields flooded by the recent rains and through the villages of Goodleigh and Lower Loxhore. During the afternoon I passed the delightfully-named Wistlandpound Reservoir, which was so hidden by the trees I could hardly catch a glimpse of the water, then on to Parracombe and back to the coast again at Lynton. Cutting inland had sliced off a big section of the coast path

43

and I'd saved myself several days but the downside was that I had missed out on some potential highlights such as Ilfracombe and the Valley of the Rocks.

It was still raining when I reached Lynton but despite the weather the place was buzzing. After the quiet of the inland lanes it came as a bit of shock to be surrounded by holidaymakers again. I'd walked about seventeen miles from Barnstaple, which felt like more than enough for the first day of the second leg, and the steep descent down the hill from Lynton to the harbour at Lynmouth felt a bit tough on my tired old legs.

When I reached the B&B I hung my wet gear up to dry in the bathroom and unpacked the rest of my kit, laying it out on the floor of my room. I'd made a few adjustments to my gear at the end of leg one and this was the first try-out of my new kit. The biggest changes were that I'd bought a new rucksack and a new pair of boots.

Before he climbed all of the 279 Munros in Scotland (hills over 3,000 feet listed by Sir Hugh Munro) in one trip, Hamish Brown didn't go out and buy a load of new kit, instead he used the gear he already had. So, apart from buying a new waterproof jacket, I'd decided to do much the same but by the end of leg one some of the cracks in the system were beginning to show. My trusty old rucksack was a massive affair with an integral steel frame and thick padded straps. It also had the less than endearing habit of filling up with water through the zips when it rained. But it was a sturdy beast, built like a tank, and had survived the tender mercies of airport baggage handlers from as far afield as Africa to Alaska. But it was also very, very heavy. It was so heavy it felt as if it was full even when it was still empty. When I got home after the first leg I carefully balanced it on the kitchen scales; it weighed more than two kilos empty. So my sturdy old, if weighty, friend

(I get ludicrously and sentimentally attached to my rucksacks) went back up into the loft whence it came and I went out and bought a super-light (and super expensive) backpack which the man in the shop told me was designed for lightweight ice climbing in the Alps. When I got home and I'd removed the straps which were designed to hold ice axes and crampons, and also several other buckles, bungy cords and dangly bits whose purpose seemed both obscure and quite unnecessary, I tried it on the scales. It weighed less than a kilo. Carrying it that first day of the second leg of the walk, even with all my kit packed inside, felt like heaven.

Apart from the blister which they had rubbed on my big toe during my misguided excursion out on Perran Beach, my old boots had been exceedingly comfortable until one sleepy afternoon, not very far out of Padstow, when the peace was disturbed by a persistent and irritating squeak which started to come from my left boot. I ignored it for a mile or two, hoping it would go away; it didn't, in fact it became worse. I can remember thinking that something must be wrong, old and well broken in boots aren't supposed to squeak. It is new boots that squeak or, as my grandmother used to say, boots which haven't been paid for. I glanced down at my left boot and it looked as if it was smiling back up at me. The sole was parting company with the uppers, opening up a wide crescent-shaped gap which looked just like a broad, toothless grin. There was nothing I could do but press on accompanied by the squeak, which was beginning to sound more and more like a tortured mouse as the afternoon wore on. As I hadn't packed a portable cobbler's kit I just had to hope it would hold together until I reached Barnstaple. So at the end of leg one of the walk I'd had to invest in a new pair of boots as well as the rucksack, and then wear the boots as much as I could to try and break them in a bit during the few weeks I had before I started on leg two.

My approach to the walk was decidedly low-tech. I had decided not to take any sort of satnav devices, GPS machines or handheld phones which can log into Google maps and will always know which direction north is. I did test out an expensive pedometer but found that the pendulum inside it tended to stick and it was less accurate than my guesswork so I abandoned that even before I started. The only technology I had was a tiny digital camera and a small mobile phone so I could text home. For navigation I used traditional maps and a compass. Looking back on the walk, I suppose I did use a bit of an eclectic combination of maps. Most of the time I stuck to the trusty Ordnance Survey Landrangers. For some of the long distance footpaths I used Harvey maps (just three maps for the whole of the Pennine Way can't be bad). When I discovered the Sustrans Cycle Routes I started using some of the Sustrans maps, which were very useful in the Midlands and the Scottish Borders. There was one occasion when I managed for several miles navigating by a sketch map on the back of an envelope and once with a page I'd torn out of Sarah's road atlas. After my expensive pedometer failed I bought an orange plastic map measurer for less than three quid from our local Yeoman's camping shop and that did a great job of working out how far I'd walked.

For me there is a ratio of happiness to misery depending on how light or how heavy my backpack is. A heavy pack can take the edge off a good day's walk so throughout the walk I worked hard at keeping my rucksack as light as possible.

For walking during the day I wore a pair of cropped walking trousers with the legs rolled up to just below the knees. These were a compromise between shorts and longs.

They were short enough for the air to get around the legs, which was great on warm days, and long enough to roll down until they met the tops of my socks, which was necessary more than once when I found myself wading through a field of stinging nettles. They had two big cargo pockets, one on each thigh, which were deep enough to hold a map in one and a notebook and pencil in the other. They were treated with some technical substance which helped them repel water, which meant they dried really quickly; they'd even dry off when it was still drizzling. On top I'd wear a lightweight shirt, I carried three of these altogether. If it was chilly I'd pull on a sleeveless wool slipover, if it was really cold I also had a fleece. I had a super-lightweight waterproof jacket and overtrousers and they did a great job of keeping me warm and dry.

For the evenings I had a pair of thin poly-cotton trousers that I'd bought in Vietnam at one of those tailors who measure you up, then make them overnight for you to pick up the next day. I usually kept one shirt for 'best' so I wasn't too sweaty and horrible in the evenings and I had a pair of thin beach shoes and a pair of ordinary black socks, so while I was never going to win the title of 'Best Dressed Man of the Year', when I was scrubbed up I looked quite decent. You could have taken me anywhere.

There was of course the ever present problem of how to keep my clothes clean. John Merrill famously walked right around the coast of Britain taking just one shirt and only washing it once. I could always 'rinse a few things through' in the sink, but I was never really very good at this. There does tend to be a bit of a gender divide here. Girls are always keen on 'rinsing things through', and they festoon the bathroom with dripping underwear; lads much less so. For me conditions had to be right before I'd set on and do some washing – that would mean a youth hostel with a good drying room or a B&B with a heated towel rail. I much preferred to use a modified version of the Hindmarsh Principle.

I first met Mr Hindmarsh at Eskdale Youth Hostel in the Lake District back sometime in the mid-1970s. He was a tall, bulky man, balding, with a friendly smile and chatty disposition. I suppose he would have been in his mid-fifties back then. I remember he told me that he worked as a customs officer and how he could spot drug smugglers just by looking into their eyes. The eyes of drug smugglers are, apparently, cloudy and have pinpoint pupils. He checked my eyes carefully and declared me drug free.

Mr Hindmarsh, or more specifically his approach to packing, was my first encounter with what the media later started calling the 'throw-away-culture'. Like me Mr Hindmarsh did not go in for 'rinsing a few things through' in the sink. Before he set off on a walking trip he would visit his local Oxfam shop and buy half a dozen regular men's type shirts, the sort you might wear with a tie if you worked in an office. They only cost him a few pence each. He would take them home, wash and iron them, and then wear his Oxfam shirts on his walking trip. When one of the shirts became a bit grubby, he'd simply throw it away and dig a clean one out of his rucksack. He'd start a trip with a full rucksack and end it with an empty one. The day I met him in Eskdale was a particularly wet one. It had poured from early morning and, as he was due to go home the next day, I can remember him donating his last clean, dry Oxfam shirt to a poor bedraggled youth hosteller who arrived soaking wet and hadn't anything dry to put on.

I didn't go to the Oxfam shop and buy shirts like Mr Hindmarsh did because I had a load of old shirts that I'd worn for work and which, since I'd been made redundant, I no longer needed. They were too old and tatty to wear for best and I'd already got more than enough shirts to wear for doing DIY or gardening. So I'd start out with a couple of 'Hindmarsh shirts' in my pack, which would be worn for a few days until they were grubby then I'd just bin them. On some of the longer legs of the walk I'd arrange for a parcel of goodies, maps and a couple more 'Hindmarsh shirts' to be sent to me along the way.

I carried a few other bits and pieces: a sunhat, water bottle, sponge bag, an aspirin or two and some plasters. Everything lived inside a waterproof kitbag in my rucksack and I also had a nylon pack cover which I used in the rain. A freak gust of wind once blew it off near Widemouth Bay and I was lucky to be able to catch it before it disappeared over the cliffs. After that I learnt to clip it to a karabiner and it never escaped very far again.

By the second leg of the walk I'd more or less got my gear right and didn't change it very much for the rest of the walk. I tried to save weight wherever I could but didn't go as far as chopping my toothbrush handle in two or cutting the labels out of my underpants. Changing my rucksack to a lightweight one and generally pruning my gear down had made a big difference. I finally knew I'd got my kit right when I was near the Scottish border staying at a remote farm deep in the Cheviots. They were used to Pennine Way walkers staying with them, staggering in weighed down under massive backpacks. I'd left my rucksack by the front door while I went into the kitchen for a cup of tea with the farmer. He was a big man, built like a wrestler, with broad shoulders and huge belly hanging over his belt. After our tea he said he'd show me my room.

'I'll bring your bag,' he said and, reaching down, he lifted it up by the straps in a hand the size of a ham. He weighed it there for a second or two and then nodded at me. 'By gum, lad,' he said, 'that's light.'

A Long Day's Journey into Bridgwater

The end of the South West Coast Path, when I reached Minehead, came as something of a shock. I'd had it alongside of me since Land's End and the thought of it not being there left me feeling strangely bereft. I'd be the first to admit that I'd not exactly been a constant companion. I had been unfaithful, I'd played fast and loose with its favours and generally wandered away from its paths of righteousness whenever the temptation took me. But, like the end of any less than satisfactory relationship, when it comes to a close you realise just how much you're going to miss its chilly comforts. I'd have to make my own way in the future and I found myself wondering how I'd cope out there, all on my own. Okay so I wasn't being sent off out into the community totally alone and without some sort of a safety net. I would be swapping the South West Coast Path for something called the West Somerset Coast Path but who's ever heard of that? No, it just wouldn't be the same. I sulked all the way to my B&B.

Next morning I followed the coast path between the shingle beach and the golf course. It was a Saturday morning and there seemed to be plenty going on. A water skier was going through his best tricks out to sea and landward steam trains regularly chugged past on the West Somerset Railway. Just beyond Blue Anchor Bay I had to scratch around a bit to find the path, which had been diverted inland and through a small wood where the coastal path had eroded away.

By early afternoon I arrived at Watchet and went to sit on the harbour wall. Harbours always look their best when the tide is in and all the boats are bobbing nicely in the water. Unfortunately for me the tide was out so I sat on the harbour wall looking at an expanse of grey-green mud.

The tide must have been in when Samuel Taylor Coleridge stopped by in 1797, accompanied by his friends William and Dorothy Wordsworth. It started out as a bit of a joint effort but finally they left it to Coleridge to complete the job of composing his most famous poem 'The Rime of the Ancient Mariner'.

I liked to consider that the walk from Watchet to Bridgwater was made up of three, not very even, parts. The first part was four miles of more or less level walking along the lanes from Watchet, through Doniford and on to the start of the Quantock Hills. This was a bit like a warm-up for the main event. Then, after a short, steep climb to the top of the ridge, I followed the Pack Way, a broad path along the whole length of the Quantocks. And then finally the third section, a drop down off the hills to Aisholt Common and a long, six mile trudge through quiet lanes to Bridgwater.

I'd set off from Watchet with the dire warnings of the B&B owner ringing in my ears. 'The lanes between Watchet and the Quantocks,' he told me, 'are extremely dangerous, because the big wagons and juggernauts speed through and use them as a shortcut'. Then he handed me a banana, wished me well and pushed me out through the front door.

I was bit rattled by this but really there was no other way to go. At the first rumble of a distant engine I'd get off the road and flatten myself against the dry stone wall until the danger had passed. But I soon realised this was a bit over the top because it was early on Sunday morning and the only traffic I saw on the lanes through Doniford and on towards West Quantoxhead was a Nissan Micra with four elderly ladies inside who looked as if they might be on their way to church, and a chap who bid me 'Good morning' as he peddled past on a bike. I arrived at the foot of the Quantocks in one piece and just in time for a downpour of rain.

There were ponies on the hills and, but for these, it would have been easy to imagine I was back in Derbyshire, especially with the rain. The Quantocks are a line of hills running roughly west to southeast. With the heather in full bloom they took on a hazy purple hue dotted with highlights of brilliant yellow where the gorse bushes were in flower. There is an old country saying that it's only when the gorse is in bloom that kissing is in season. But romantics need have no cause to fret because the gorse is one of the few plants which blooms all the year around. Despite the gorse I wasn't planning on doing any kissing any time soon. There was nobody around to snog for one thing and anyway I didn't have the breath for it, not as I laboured up to the top of the Pack Way.

After the rain the weather brightened and I had clear views back the way I'd come. I could see Watchet with its tiny harbour (now full of water) and, back along the coast, in the distance I could see the sun catching on the white peaks of the Butlin's camp at Minehead. I took a long last look out to sea because this was the point the walk turned inland and the next time I would look out to sea proper would be the Firth of Forth on the east coast of Scotland. Then I turned around, pointed my boots inland and trudged off.

There wasn't much danger of getting lost on the hogs-back of the Quantocks but there were plenty of smaller paths branching off in all directions. I'd seventeen miles to cover before Bridgwater and I didn't want to lose time drifting off down one of the side routes so, in fair weather and superb visibility, I took the first compass bearing of the entire trip, just to keep me on the straight and narrow.

At the far end of the ridge near the Triscombe Stone I did make a short detour back out across the open moor to climb Wills Neck, the highest point of the Quantock Hills and the highest point of the walk so far. I took a break on the summit and ate the banana from the B&B while the ponies grazed all around me.

I passed several more groups of ponies, some with well-grown foals, as I walked down the 'Slades' and along the edge of a plantation. Where the path became a metalled road I stopped to watch two crows as they mobbed a buzzard, then they chased it off in the direction of Aisholt Common.

Part three of the day's walk consisted of a muscle-crunching six miles along back roads, past Hawkridge Reservoir and through Spaxton village. In the lay-by alongside the reservoir at least a dozen cars were pulled in facing the water, but not one of the white-haired occupants of the cars were looking out at the view, all of them had their noses buried deep in the Sunday papers. They didn't look up from the colour supplements when I walked past and not even when a huge trout jumped clear of the water only a few yards out and landed back again with a loud splash. There was even an ice cream van parked in the lay-by to cater for them, but the chap inside just gazed into space and moodily picked at his teeth. Nobody was eating ice creams.

It was late afternoon when I reached Bridgwater and found my digs in the outbuildings of the old vicarage. My room looked out onto a walled garden with formal flowerbeds and climbing roses where a black cat padded around its domain before jumping onto the wall, curling up and going to sleep.

One of the great things about walking Land's End to John

O'Groats (or vice versa) is that you have a start point and an end point but your route, and what you get up to in-between, is entirely your own affair (providing it is legal of course, between consenting adults and you don't frighten the horses). Unlike the South West Coast Path and most other long distance paths there is no 'official' route to follow and even if you occasionally have to endure the frowns of disapproval from other walkers when you veer off an 'approved route' this freedom is to be valued. I found the best policy was to smile sweetly at them and just carry on. Don't attempt to explain. And long may this freestyle and unregulated state of affairs remain. But if there is an exception to every rule then when it comes to freestyle End to Ending the town of Bridgwater is that exception. It's a place you just can't avoid as your route takes you from the southwest and on into the Somerset Levels. The need to cross first the River Parrett and then the M5 motorway means that it is an unwritten law that sooner or later even the most individualistic End to Enders find their freestyle and independent footsteps will take them on a long day's journey all the way to Bridgwater.

Bubblegum Toothpaste

It was in Bridgwater that all of my efforts to cut down the weight of my rucksack sort of backfired. Standing in the bathroom, I was only able to squeeze the tiniest smear of minty-flavoured fluoride-rich toothpaste onto my brush from the micro holiday-sized tube I'd packed, and the next day was August Bank Holiday Monday, when all the shops would be shut. End to End walking can be a pretty solitary affair but even so I didn't want to be Halitosis Harry or Dr Dog-breath all the way to Bath so, next morning before I left town, I took a walk along the main shopping street. I was in luck, the 99p Shop was open and, what's more, they sold toothpaste.

The toiletries section wasn't extensive and they only had big family-sized tubes of toothpaste. I picked one up and weighed it in my hand. It was nearly as heavy as my spare set of clothes. I put it back on the shelf. A bit further along, next to the shampoo, there was a section of stuff for kids and there, hidden behind teddy bear-shaped sponges and rubber ducks for bathtime, was a Garfield the Cat Travel Kit. Fixed to a card and wrapped in plastic was a little ginger-coloured toothbrush with its own travel cover. It had a holographic picture of Garfield on the front (so his image stood up or sat down when you rocked it backwards and forwards) and a tiny tube of Garfield's special toothpaste, bubblegum flavour. I rushed to the tills and paid for it with a pound coin and was given a penny change. I tried out Garfield's bubblegum toothpaste that evening when I reached the youth hostel. It came out of the tube the texture of putty and was a deep aquamarine blue, like the colour of tropical seas in the travel brochures, and it tasted so sweet it made my toes curl. It was nothing like any gum I'd ever blown bubbles with. More like the sticky saccharine-flavoured sweets we used to call torpedoes, which I could remember finding at the bottom of lucky bags when I was a kid. But I didn't have any alternative, I had to use it to clean my teeth with until I reached Bath.

With my Garfield the Cat Travel Kit safely packed in my rucksack it seemed a long walk through the suburbs of Bridgwater. When I reached the edge of town I took a path across a field to reach the footbridge over the M5 motorway. Judging by the evidence on the ground, this was the favourite walk for the town's dog owners. From my vantage point on the bridge, and with the traffic speeding past below me, I was able to spy out the land ahead. The path disappeared into a field of yellow maize stalks, each about seven feet high, and each field was edged not with a wall or a fence but, this being the Somerset Levels, a wide drainage ditch. About three quarters of a mile ahead there was another footbridge, this one went over a particularly broad ditch, and beyond that was the church tower in the village of Chedzoy, which was the landmark I was aiming for. I could see that with the tall maize the map wasn't going to be a lot of use, it was going to be more like a memory test. I tried to fix the lay of the land in my mind then I plunged off into the deep maize.

Even as a kid I was never very good at memory games and ten minutes into the maize I had totally forgotten the grid pattern of drainage ditches and I wasn't even sure if I was going in the right direction. It was like descending into another world. The maize (or should I say maze) had grown a couple of feet taller than the top of my head. It seemed to absorb or blot out all sound, even the noise of the motorway traffic, and replace it with its own whispery soft rattling sound as it moved gently in the breeze. It would have been quite soothing if I hadn't been totally lost. Visibility was about two feet in any direction, or as close as the nearest stalks of maize. The only way I could make any progress was to work my way around the edges of the fields, which added another hazard to my list of woes because the field edges were choked with nettles and brambles.

After struggling on for what seemed like an hour I came to a small gap in the vegetation and peered through. I could see a bridge and the church beyond, and it was the bridge I had been aiming for. It didn't seem very far away but between me and it was a very wide ditch filled with very black-looking water.

I backtracked through the nettles to see if I could find a crossing place but there was nowhere which looked very promising. I was damned if I was going back all the way to the motorway bridge (I wasn't even sure I could find it anyway), there had to be a way through. Ten minutes of searching and I found a potential crossing place. By potential crossing place I don't mean the sort of place any normal, sane person would consider trying to cross. I mean a potential crossing place for a desperate End to End walker who is hot, nettled, angry and close to panicking. An End to End walker who knows he's still got at least fifteen miles to go before he gets to the youth hostel at Street and who can see the morning vanishing fast because he's wasted too much time wandering around lost in a field full of maize and in the 99p Shop buying silly novelty toothpaste.

The first task was to find out where solid ground ended and ditch began. This wasn't as easy as it sounds because the bank at my side was a dense mat of brambles and nettles, and the far bank was slick mud. The water was fetid with green algae floating on the top. I had no way of telling how deep it was. There wasn't much on my bank to hang on to, just a stunted hawthorn bush which looked as if it would struggle to support a decent-sized sparrow, but I didn't have much choice but to trust my weight to it and lean out over the water making frantic stabbing motions at the far bank with my trekking pole. At the second prod the spike on the end stuck in the mud and I was suspended over the dark waters with the twiggy hawthorn bush in one hand and the spindly aluminium telescopic trekking pole in the other. I was poised in no-man's-land trying to remember if I'd tightened the pole up properly before I'd left Bridgwater. The next problem was summoning the courage to make the jump for the far bank. A soaking in those dark waters would be the price of getting my timing wrong. I knew I couldn't hang about there all day and when cramp started to spread down my left arm and I could feel the trekking pole slowly beginning to telescope back into itself I knew I couldn't put the fateful moment off any longer. Screwing up what bit of energy I had left, I went for it. Something between a lunge and a pole vault. It wasn't pretty and it wasn't elegant. I wouldn't have won any points for style or technique but I made it. Or rather ninety-five percent of me made it. My right foot went under and came out dripping and covered with pond weed. I stood on the far bank feeling surprised I was there at all, then set off and squelched all the rest of the way into Chedzoy.

I'd planned to walk along King's Sedgemoor Drain heading southeast but although my map and guidebook told me this was a great walk, on the ground there was just overgrown banks with chained and padlocked access gates; yet another virtual footpath. There was a lovely path along the drain in the other direction where people were walking, cycling and fishing, but that didn't help me a great deal. After my earlier encounter with the giant maize field and the waterlogged ditch my sense of adventure was at an all-time low and my foot still hadn't dried out so there was nothing to do but hoof it along the road and try and make up some lost time.

I walked past more fields of maize, more drainage ditches and at one point startled a buzzard perched on a low branch beside the road. It spread its wings, laboured into the air then flew across the flat Somerset countryside, mewing as it went.

By early afternoon I reached one of those small country pubs tucked away in the middle of nowhere. The sort of place you can never find again, even if you go back to look for it. I'd arrived just in time to watch the final of their annual August Bank Holiday Monday Wheelbarrow Races.

In teams of two, the local lads took turns pushing and riding in a wheelbarrow, in a sprint downhill to a stream at the bottom, where they turned around and raced back up the hill. To make it a test of skill as well as brute force the lad sitting in the wheelbarrow had to hold two tall paper cups brimming with water. As well as winning the race, the aim was to still have two cups full of water when they crossed the finish line outside the pub.

The whole village seemed to have turned out and quite a crowd had clustered around the pub doorway, where an elderly gent wearing red braces and a green eyeshade sat at a table taking bets.

The finalists set off down the hill at a cracking pace. We all craned our necks to see them turn at the bottom but on the run-in it looked as if a bit of pushing and shoving was going on and the favourite was beaten by half a wheelbarrow's length. The money was on the loser and there were dark murmurings from amongst the crowd. A tall, sandy-haired man at the back called for a steward's enquiry and there was talk of a rematch.

I took a few photos of the races then tried to make my way into the pub to buy a drink but there seemed to have been something of a sea change in the mood since the end of the last race. It felt as if a storm cloud had passed in front of the sun. I don't know if the locals thought I was something of a wheelbarrow racing tout, or maybe they just didn't like rucksack-toting End to Enders, but the crowd bunched up around the pub door, and nobody seemed to want to move up to let me get in. When I did get into the public bar the conversation stopped abruptly as I walked in and I ordered my drink amid silence and dark stares. I took my beer to one of the tables and sat down on my own. Some small children had been playing noisily in the bar when I entered but their mothers called them back and gathered them into their arms then sat scowling in my direction while the men folk stood at the bar and glared at me. It was all beginning to feel a bit like *Deliverance*; if anyone had produced a banjo I would have been off down the road like a shot. As it was, a youth in a baseball cap and nylon shellsuit went over to the jukebox and put on some loud rap music. That was enough for me. I drained my beer, put my rucksack back on and left the pub. Just as I was going the old guy in the braces announced to the crowd that they'd raised fifty pounds for the village's 'Friendship Fund'.

It was turning into an eventful day but it wasn't over yet. After ditch-leaping at Chezdoy, nonexistent paths along King's Sedgemoor Drain and wheelbarrow races outside the pub, I was looking forward to an afternoon's gentle walk down the Somerset lanes to the youth hostel. I arrived in the village of Street at four in the afternoon and took a wander around the town, thinking that I was bound to come across the hostel sooner or later. After all, Street isn't a very big place. But there was no sign of the youth hostel. The tourist information office was open, so I called in to see if they could give me directions.

When I first used to go hostelling back in the 1970s the Youth Hostels Association (YHA) produced a useful handbook every year which listed all of the hostels *and* gave directions, along with a little sketch map. I'm a life member of the YHA but hadn't been hostelling for twenty years before I set off on my End to End walk. Along with the other 'improvements' which had taken place during that time, the handbooks and helpful little sketch maps

60

with directions to the hostels had vanished and a recurring problem I had found on my walk was that I'd arrive at my destination at the end of a long day's walk and spend a weary half hour tramping around the place trying to find the youth hostel or B&B where I was due to stay.

Whenever you ask for directions there are two phrases that you just don't want to hear: 'you don't need the map' and 'you can't miss it'. The lady in the tourist information office was most helpful.

'The youth hostel?' she said. 'Oh that's easy, you don't need the map. You go down the main road, turn right at the Bear Inn, past the open-air swimming pool, down the road, turn right, then left and you can't miss it.'

So I thanked her, went out to the main road, right at the Bear Inn, past the open-air swimming pool and walked down the road leading out of town. And I walked, and I walked and I walked. I walked until I started to get that fretful feeling that I'd gone wrong somewhere along the line. There was no youth hostel. There wasn't anything else, for that matter. No sign of any kind of habitation, just the road with hawthorn hedges on each side and hay fields beyond them. I studied the map. Youth hostels are shown as a tiny red triangle on Ordnance Survey maps. I scrutinised the area all around Street; there was a line of little red diamonds marking the Samaritans Way, but I couldn't see a little red triangle anywhere. The youth hostel must still exist. I knew a lot of hostels had closed but I was sure Street was still in business because I'd phoned up and spoken to the warden only a week or so before. I'd even arranged for a parcel of goodies and some 'Hindmarsh' spare clothes to be sent there for me.

I'd passed a left turn on the way out of town but not a right turn; had the woman in the tourist office mixed up her left and right or had I misheard? I decided to turn around and walk back into town and ask the next person I met.

After three quarters of a mile I met a young chap walking an Old English Sheepdog. He wasn't sure but thought if I went, left, right and right again it might be there. I followed his directions. First of all I passed some substantial houses surrounded by lawns and well-kept gardens. They gave way to smaller houses, flats, a nursing home and a football pitch. It was now late on a bank holiday Monday and Street was sleepily quiet, with nobody about to ask. Then a woman came towards me carrying two bulging carrier bags of shopping.

'No, no,' she told me. 'You've come miles out of your way. Turn left at the bottom of this road and keep going.'

I turned left at the bottom of the road and after ten minutes found myself back in town outside the Bear Inn and the open-air swimming pool. I stood across the road from the pool listening to the shouts, the laughter and sounds of splashing from the kids playing inside. They were having fun and all sounded so happy while I was on the verge of panic. I'd reached the point where I didn't believe I'd ever find the youth hostel. Street may not be very big but I'd covered every inch of it and I was back where I'd started. Had Street Youth Hostel slipped through a black hole and was now existing in another dimension of time and space, was it rubbing shoulders out there with Dr Who and the Tardis? What worried me was that when I asked the locals, the people who *actually* lived in Street, they didn't know where it was either. They all seemed to have some vague idea that Street Youth Hostel existed, or had once existed, but they were not at all sure when or where.

A middle-aged woman came out of the entrance to the pool, her hair still wet and slicked down from the water.

She had a boy of about six holding onto one hand and in the other she was carrying a bag of wet swimming things. She seemed to have a friendly sort of face so I thought I'd give it one last go. I crossed the road and asked her if she could tell me the way to the youth hostel. A look of mild panic came into her eyes and her smile turned to a frown.

'Err, I'm not sure, dear,' she said. Then her face lit up. An idea occurred to her. 'Tell you what, go into the pool and ask for Dave. Dave might know.'

I sat down on the wall outside the pool almost ready to admit defeat. I took my pack off and dug into its depths and found my mobile phone and the youth hostel's number. I dialled the number but only got the answering machine. My shoulders slumped. Sitting outside the swimming pool listening to the merry shouts of the swimmers inside, I felt as wretched as I'd ever felt on the walk. It was the closest I'd come to blubbing. What sort of an End to Ender was I? I couldn't find a youth hostel with a map and a compass on a sunny bank holiday afternoon, how was I ever going to find my way to John O'Groats? Then my phone rang; it was the youth hostel returning my call.

'Directions to the hostel?' said the warden. 'No problem. You don't need the map just turn right at the Bear Inn, past the open-air swimming pool, down the road, turn right, left and you can't miss it ...'

'Look,' I said, 'I've tried that, I've been there, I've covered every inch of the town, I can't even see it on the map.'

'Well,' he said in a very patient voice, 'it is there on the map, but you've got to know where to look. The little red triangle sort of gets mixed up with all the little red diamonds from the Samaritans Way.'

Then he said the magic words, '... *but it's quite a long*

way from town, further than you'd think, it's going to take you at least half an hour to walk.'

'Thank you,' I said. I felt as if all of the world's troubles had just been lifted from my shoulders. 'I'll see you in half an hour.'

'I'll have the kettle on,' said the warden.

Forgive Us Our Trespasses

It was going to just be a short walk, five miles or so, from Street to Glastonbury. At least I knew I wouldn't have similar problems finding where I was staying in Glastonbury because I was indulging myself with a night at the George and Pilgrims. Built in the fifteenth century to provide accommodation for pilgrims visiting the abbey, the George and Pilgrims claimed to be the oldest pub in the Southwest. It was the sort of ancient inn you wouldn't have felt out of place riding up to the front door on your white charger, dropping off your shield and lance by the main reception and clanking up the stairs still in your chain mail. If I couldn't quite compete with an entrance like that I could content myself with the thought that I was a guest on a quest. Okay, nothing as grand as a mission to slay a fire-breathing dragon, and not even in the same league as seeking the Holy Grail, but as quests go, walking End to End would have to do for the time being.

The walk from Street to Glastonbury was uneventful apart from meeting two riders a couple of miles from Street. I was minding my own business and admiring the view of Glastonbury Tor, when two ladies on horseback, resplendent in their hard hats and hacking jackets, cantered up from behind. One of the horses, even to my untrained eye, seemed a bit fractious. He was tossing his head and making as much progress sideways as forward. His eyes were wild and rolled around in his head and dark patches of sweat showed through his otherwise glossy coat. The rider was trying to keep him on a tight rein but the horse wasn't having any of it.

'I'm awfully sorry,' she said, as the horse skittered up behind me, 'but would you mind talking to my horse as I ride past you.'

'I'm sorry,' I said. 'Did you say you wanted me to … ?'

'Yes, that's right. Talk to my horse. Please.'

'Well yes but …'

'He's a bit neurotic you see and passing people scares him. He doesn't mind cars and lorries and things but he doesn't like people very much. If you'll just talk to him he'll calm down.'

'Err, right, okay. What sort of thing would he like me to talk about?'

'Oh anything will do. Tell him a joke or something.'

'Right, well, has he heard the one about the white horse who goes into a pub and asks for a double whisky?'

'Yes of course he's heard that one, look I do wish you'd take this seriously. I don't want to end up in the ditch. He's in a particularly bad mood this morning.'

'Sorry. Well does he know what's brown and skims across the water at sixty miles an hour?' They had drawn alongside me by this point.

'Never mind, he doesn't like jokes much anyway.'

'He's not called Mr Ed is he?' I said. 'Remember, the talking horse who used to be on TV?'

'No,' she said looking down her nose at me from on high. 'He's called Eric.'

I left my rucksack at the George and Pilgrims and walked

down the main street. Glastonbury is the hippie capital of England. The scent of smouldering joss sticks drifted out through the shop doorways and if I'd wanted to indulge there was every kind of enlightenment and spiritual healing on offer: Pagan, Ying and Yang, Wiccan. I'd only missed out on the Goddess Conference by a few days. In the window of the shop selling crystals was a sign which read: 'If you shoplift we may just turn you into stone.'

Glastonbury must have done something to awake the ageing hippie within me: I had vegetarian quiche for lunch, a glass of carrot juice and spent the afternoon drifting around the abbey grounds in a sort of chilled out haze.

After an easy walk from Street to Glastonbury I was expecting the walk to Radstock to be more of a trudge.

I'd planned my routes so that most of my End to End walk was through country which was new to me. As a general rule I tried to link together some of the established long distance walking routes because they promised to be good walking, to avoid built-up areas and to keep roadwalking to a minimum. Also; these trails tended to have decent networks of accommodation and B&Bs. I didn't plan to camp at all. Not unless I really couldn't avoid it. Lugging along a tent, sleeping bag and all the other gubbins makes camping a drag. And anyway, it always rains when I go camping.

My overall route had been to start off by broadly following the South West Coast Path from Land's End to Minehead and by the time I'd reached Glastonbury I was working my way across country, aiming for Bath and the start of the Cotswold Way. Where there was no suitable long distance trail I got the maps out and came up with my own route as best I could, trying to stick to footpaths or minor roads. I discovered the route I was following from

Glastonbury to Radstock coincided with Sustrans Cycle Route 3.

After Bath it would be mostly following the Cotswold Way to Chipping Camden then I was planning to head more or less due north, following cycle routes and canal towpaths up through the Midlands. This would take me through more built-up areas but for me the walk was about experiencing the changing landscape as I worked my way up through Britain, so the canals of Birmingham and the back streets of Walsall were as much a part of my End to End walk as the sea cliffs of Cornwall or the high moors of the Pennines.

After the Midlands I would work my way through my home county of Derbyshire to join the Pennine Way at Edale. I'd wanted to walk the Pennine Way since I was a lad but somehow it had never happened. The layman sees the Pennine Way as a sort of benchmark which sorts out the serious walker from the lightweight. It doesn't matter what other feats of endurance you may have done, from Bill Cowley's Lyke Wake Walk to the Inca Trail in darkest Peru, if you haven't bog-trotted your way up the Pennines you simply don't cut the mustard.

The Pennine Way should see me north of the border then it would be a case of picking my way through the industrial belt around Glasgow and Edinburgh. This was easier than it first appeared. Cherry-picking bits of the Border Abbeys Way, St Cuthbert's Way and some of the old drove roads should see me to Edinburgh. From there, amazingly, a canal towpath should get me almost all the way to Milngavie just outside Glasgow and the start of the West Highland Way. Ninety miles of West Highland Way to Fort William (which doesn't sound much if I say it quickly) and then follow the Great Glen Way to Inverness. Once this far north the options become a bit more limited and it is increasingly impossible to avoid long stretches of roadwalking, especially that road most detested by the End to Ender, the A9. But once the A9 was behind me it should be pleasant back roads through to John O'Groats itself. Easy.

But all of this was a long way ahead and still in the realms of being an End to End walker's fantasy as I left Glastonbury on Cycle Route 3, which was conveniently screened from the busy A39 by a hedge. I turned off just beyond Hartlake Bridge and followed a long, straight and featureless lane flanked on each side by water-filled ditches. I saw more birdlife than traffic; two herons and three moorhens trumps two cyclists and a white van.

As lunchtime approached it was clear that I was coming to the end of the Somerset Levels. Near Launcherly there was a range of low hills and I had a view of Wells Cathedral off to my left.

My map showed a small lane leading to the church in Dinder Village. Ideal, I thought, it would avoid some roadwalking along the A371. It started much like any other lane but after half a mile it began to look tidier and a whole lot better kept than the average country lane. Then I went over a very smart-looking bridge with carved stone balustrades and beyond that there was a maze cut into the turf. It was all beginning to look a bit country house-ish. A chap wearing blue overalls, a hard hat, safety goggles and ear protectors and carrying an industrial-strength grass strimmer was walking purposefully in my direction. I've always been taught that it's best to get your excuses in first.

'Am I trespassing?' I shouted at him.

'What?' he yelled.

'Am I ...'

'Just a minute,' he said, and cut the motor on the strimmer and lifted up his ear protectors.

'Am I trespassing?'

'Yes, you are,' he said, 'this is private property.'

'Oh. Sorry about that.'

'Where are you trying to get to?'

'Dinder village, the map shows a lane leading to the church. I didn't know it was private.'

He was pretty decent about it, all things considered. He told me that if I went back over the bridge, and followed the river through the field, I would come to a footpath which joined the road just before Dinder. So I managed to avoid the A371 but with the bit of mild trespassing it took me twice as long to reach the village.

The afternoon was a trudge through featureless lanes with just two highlights. The Red Arrows Aerobatics Team flew over in formation. I saw on the news later that night that they had gone to do an air display over Weston-super-Mare to cheer the townspeople up after the pier had been burnt down. And later I was able to cut off a corner of roadwalking by taking a footpath through the ancient Maesbury Castle. There was no castle as such but a substantial earth mound surrounded by a ditch. In the middle it was hollowed into a bowl shape where a herd of Friesian cattle stopped their grazing long enough to watch me walk past.

I stayed overnight at a pub in Radstock and next morning followed Cycle Route 24 along the Collier's Way. I went by way of Wellow, Monkton Comb and finally, I climbed over the ridge and dropped down into Bath.

The City of Bath was under siege by an invasion of glass fibre pigs. It all started with the Cow Parades, outdoor art events where decorated glass fibre cows started appearing all over the place. There had been Cow Parades in London, Edinburgh and Manchester. These inspired similar events around the country but with different kinds of glass fibre animals. There had been bears and baby elephants and, in Bath, King Bladud's pigs.

In 863 BC Prince Bladud contracted leprosy (this is the point in the story where you should be prepared to suspend disbelief). He was driven out of town and told to look after the pigs. This was not a wise move on the part of the City Fathers because the pigs caught leprosy from him. Then one bright morning he found his pigs having a wallow in a pool of hot water and mud and, being an observant man, he noticed that the waters of this pungent and steamy pool had cured the pigs of their leprosy. You can imagine the whoop of gay abandon as he flung off his doublet and hose, jumped in beside his pigs and was also cured. So he went back home, they made him king, he founded the City of Bath and set up a thriving tourist trade marketing its health-giving waters.

Reaching Bath was the end of the Southwest section of the walk and a significant milestone, one which I felt called for an appropriate, if modest, celebration. So with a respectful nod in the direction of King Bladud, I went into the nearest greasy spoon and treated myself to a bacon sandwich.

PART TWO – THE ENGINE ROOM

Horses for Courses

There are some things which weigh heavily on the mind of the End to Ender as he or she takes those first tentative steps away from the signpost at Land's End. They worry about fitness, they worry about endurance and they worry about getting lost. They fret about navigation, about bad weather and about blisters. But all of these concerns pale into insignificance beside the biggest worry of all: where will they find to lay their weary head at the end of each long day's walk?

A lot of End to Enders will opt to take a tent. There's something very comforting about carrying your home, carapace-like, with you wherever you go. And cost alone makes camping an attractive option. Make no mistake, walking Land's End to John O'Groats is an expensive business. You can count on between two to three months on the road. That's two to three months not at work or earning any money, but you will still need feeding (boy will you need feeding) and you will need housing. Then there are incidentals which quickly add up, the new gear you will have to buy, the guidebooks and the maps. I used more than thirty maps of one sort or another. Camping may be the cheapest option but, quite apart from campsite fees, which are not cheap, it has its drawbacks. Your pack, even with the latest hi-tech, super-lightweight gear, will be heavy, very heavy. And at the end of a day's walk you have to set on and pitch camp, usually in the rain, and there is nowhere to dry wet clothes inside your little nylon home from home. What's more, when you have pitched your tent, often in a field where you are surrounded by large, flatulent and inquisitive animals, each one sporting a big set of pointy horns, it can be surprisingly hard to get a good night's sleep. I was a keen camper in my teens and early twenties but as the years passed, and early retirement loomed, the lure of life under canvas became less and less attractive, especially compared to the delights of a warm bed, under a proper roof, preferably after a hot meal and a pint or two of beer. I have carried out extensive research into the accounts of walkers who set out to camp End to End and my findings are that the further they go, the less they camp and the more they are tempted into B&Bs. And who would blame them? The prospect of finding somewhere to camp after a mammoth day's walk, putting up the tent in a howling gale, heating a dehydrated meal over a camping stove before turning in to a damp sleeping bag when, just down the road, there is a welcoming pub or a cosy B&B, well there's just no comparison. My original thought that evening, when I first decided to walk from End to End, was followed a nanosecond later with the thought that there was no way on earth that I was going to camp.

The original plan was to stay in youth hostels and make up any gaps in the network with bunk houses, camping barns and B&Bs. This didn't work out because there simply were just not enough youth hostels, or at least not where I needed them. In practice I stayed at a few youth hostels but mostly in B&Bs, small hotels and pubs. This was expensive, very expensive, so much so that I have resisted ever totting up how much the whole darn thing cost me. It would be just too upsetting. But was there ever a man enjoyed frittering his redundancy money more than I?

Where the walk was concerned I planned to take a leaf out of Robert Louis Stevenson's book (specifically his essay on 'Walking Tours' in *Virginibus Puerisque*). I wouldn't be an 'over-walker'. One who covers an 'unconscionable distance', each day, 'merely to stupefy and brutalise himself'. I would be what he referred to as a 'temperate walker'. Not, I should quickly add, to be confused with an alcohol abstaining 'temperance' walker. A temperate walker, according to RLS, is one who 'cannot tell whether he puts his knapsack on, or takes it off, with more delight. The excitement of the departure puts him in key for that of the arrival'. I decided I would aim to temperately walk fourteen miles each day. That's not too much for an old timer, but far enough to keep the miles ticking over. Where this theory started to unravel was that suitable places to stay were seldom at neat fourteen mile intervals. So some days I found myself walking a lot more miles than I really wanted to, and occasionally, very occasionally, a lot less.

In order to stick to my fourteen-mile average as closely as I could, and to make sure I had somewhere to stay at the end of each day, I booked my accommodation way ahead, before I set out on each leg of the walk, and it was this, seemingly trivial task, that was by far the most irksome of the whole enterprise.

At the end of the previous stage of the walk, and during a short break from pig-spotting in Bath, I'd dropped into the Tourist Information office and bought an accommodation guide for the Cotswold Way, which was to be the next leg of the walk. And so, on a bleak morning in January, when the wind was throwing handfuls of sleet against the window, I sat down at home in the warm with my accommodation guide, the map, a telephone and a newly-sharpened pencil to book my accommodation for the next leg of the walk.

I started by phoning the first B&B on the list. There

was no answer. I tried the next one. The phone rang twice and then clicked through to a mobile. A man answered and said he was in the bank, but he promised to call me back the instant he got home. He never phoned back. I tried ringing him later but his phone was constantly engaged. I called the next B&B on my list and this time I did get through.

'Hello, I'm walking the Cotswold Way in the second week in March,' I said, 'and I'd like to book for bed and breakfast.' There was a sharp intake of breath at the other end of the phone.

'Second week in March?' he said. 'Very busy then.' There was the sound of rustling paper; I assumed he was thumbing through his diary. 'No, fully booked all that week.' And the phone clicked abruptly off.

I tried the next B&B and had a similar response. I was beginning to run out of options but tried again. It was a woman who answered the phone this time but the message was the same. 'Very busy that week, fully booked.'

I can be a bit slow on the uptake at the best of times but even I was beginning to see something of a pattern here. I know the Cotswolds are very attractive, and I know they are popular, but everywhere booked up, for the second week of March? Just before she hung up I said, 'Look, am I missing something here? This is the third bed and breakfast I've phoned and they're all full, is there something going on I don't know about?'

'Of course not,' she sounded a bit huffy. 'It's just that I'm planning to have the family over that week so won't have room to do B&B, that's all.' And she rang off.

After that I had a little run of luck and managed to secure three consecutive nights of accommodation, then it reverted back to type.

'No indeed,' said the manager of a small hotel near

Chipping Sodbury. He didn't even check his diary. 'Fully booked all week and I'd imagine everywhere else will be.'

'I'm missing something aren't I?' I said. 'There's something's going on that week.'

'Yes,' he said, 'it's the National Hunt Festival at Cheltenham.'

'Oh, bugger.'

'The biggest event in the National Hunt racing calendar.'

'Oh shit, bugger, arseholes.'

'Half the population of Ireland come over to Cheltenham that week for the racing.' He was starting to enjoy himself. 'Every B&B, hotel and guesthouse for miles around will be booked solid.'

'Well thank you anyway,' I said, 'and sorry about the bad language.'

'Think nothing of it. People book up from one year to the next, you know, we all have a great week.'

'It sounds wonderful.'

'Oh yes it is, shame you'll be missing it.'

Shame indeed, I was stuck with bookings for the first half of the Cotswold Way and what looked like little prospect of booking anywhere for the second half. There was nothing for it but to turn back to my accommodation guide and keep on trying.

I'd nearly chewed my pencil down to a stub and my accommodation guide was full of more crosses than ticks but I was slowly making progress. Then it came to booking somewhere to stay at Cleeve Hill on the outskirts of Cheltenham itself.

'No problem,' said the chap at the end of a crackly line. I dropped my pencil and nearly dropped the phone as well. 'One person for bed and breakfast on Friday the thirteenth, Cheltenham Gold Cup Day.'

In a haze of euphoria I gave him my credit card details

to confirm the booking then just before I put the phone down he said, 'Tell me, are you a gambling man?'

'Me? Well no, not really, a couple of bob on the Grand National and the Derby maybe.'

'A lucky guy like you,' he said. 'You should go straight out to the bookies and put a big bet on the Gold Cup.'

'Me? Lucky?'

'I should say so. Back the favourite, put everything you can afford on it, and then put what you can't afford on it as well.'

'Well, if you think so. Maybe a bit of a flutter, a couple of quid each way,' said the last of the big spenders.

'Not a flutter,' he said. 'Put your shirt on it. Look, every hotel and B&B has been booked up solid for weeks. Then two minutes before you rang one of my oldest regular customers phoned to say he couldn't stay for the last day of the race meeting. I've just given you his bed. I'd say you're a lucky guy. You've just booked the last bed in Cheltenham.'

Random Tyndale and the Royal Wee

Bath Cathedral disappeared in a squall of snow and I started to wonder if the second week of March was perhaps a tad early to be setting out. Next morning was cold and clear with a brisk wind from the north. I found myself whistling a tune as I walked along Bath's famous Crescent and on out of town. It felt good to be on the road again.

The field leading up Penn Hill had been turned into a quagmire by weeks of rain and by the collective hooves of a herd of skittish bullocks. They stood around in groups of four or five, knee-deep in mire looking balefully at me, their shaggy coats spattered with mud. I was hot and gasping for breath when I reached the top of the field. The bullocks had been there as well and they had decorated the stile to match the rest of the field. They'd opted for a pebble-dashed look.

Beyond the field was a good lane which was dry underfoot and I started to make good time. I was soon to discover that most of the Cotswold Way is along lanes and bridleways of this sort. I've always enjoyed walking along lanes. I find myself imagining farm carts and hay wains from centuries past being drawn along them by heavy horses. To me they have a great sense of history and also a sense of purpose, that and, even for someone like me, it's really, really difficult to get lost when you're following a walled lane.

This one wound its way past Kelston Round Hill and onto Prospect Stile, where there was a small, sad memorial in polished marble to a Sarah Louise Gray, who had died at that spot, aged just seventeen years. A couple of miles further along there was an altogether more pretentious memorial, crowned with a rampant, if rather weathered, griffin, to a gentleman with the splendidly alliterative name of Sir Bevil Greville. He apparently came to a sticky end not very far away in 1643 during the Battle of Lansdown in the Civil War.

The Cotswold Way broadly follows the line of an escarpment north from Bath to Chipping Camden and on that first day, walking the fourteen miles from Bath to Tormarton, I had the hills to myself. Next morning I set out early through Dodington Park. March is perhaps a little too early for Cotswold Way walkers; I only had the sheep and a couple of dog walkers for company. The walk from Tormarton to North Nibley could be described as 'monumental.' Not because it was a particularly long walk (it was fifteen miles) but because I came across a dozen or more monuments and memorials of one sort or another. It was like join-the-dots walking from one commemorative edifice to another. Old Sodbury had a memorial to Queen Victoria and a war memorial incorporated into the church lychgate. Behind the church there was a seat to commemorate the Millennium, where someone had accidentally left a child's purse, decorated in pirate style with skull and crossbones, along with a half-eaten packet of Cadbury's chocolate fingers. Little Sodbury church had a plaque to William Tyndale, who came from thereabouts. He became famous in 1523 for translating the Bible into English, which sounds very worthy but also pretty dull. Not so, not back in those days, translating the Bible into English was about as risky and subversive as you could get. If the Bible was translated into English it wrested religious control away from the King and the leaders of the church because the common people were able to read for themselves what the Bible said, instead of having to follow whatever spin the ruling classes chose to put on it. And for his efforts Tyndale was persecuted and died a martyr in 1536. Incongruously, a stone close to Tyndale's was a plaque to Random Tom, a DJ who died tragically young.

There were war memorials at Hillesley, Old and Hawkesbury Upton. At Hawesbury there was the hundred foot tall Somerset Monument (to Robert Somerset, a general at Waterloo) and Wooton-under-Edge boasted a memorial clock to Queen Victoria and a walled coppice on the top of the hill to commemorate Waterloo. And, finally, dominating the skyline above the village of North Nibley, and back by popular demand, there was a massive phallic-shaped tower to William Tyndale.

I discovered that some B&B establishments, especially in the Cotswolds, seemed rather coy about advertising the fact that they offered bed and breakfast at all. If they had a

B&B sign outside it was a discreet one, some had none at all and with my ineptitude at finding places this proved a problem more than once.

Somewhere around the mid-point of the Cotswolds I pitched up late one Saturday afternoon, weary and footsore, entering the village along a quiet lane which was flanked each side by rustic stone cottages, most of which were topped with thatched roofs. They were all neat and well-kept, surrounded by trimmed beech hedges and tidy herbaceous borders. It was the sort of place where something as vulgar as a B&B sign would totally spoil the effect and put them right out of the running for next year's best kept village award. Pleasing on the eye maybe but finding my digs quickly became a process of trial and error. I knocked tentatively on the front door of the house I hoped was the right one. The door moved slightly when I knocked. I had the impression that it wasn't closed properly and certainly not locked. After two minutes of knocking there was no answer. I tried around the back. There was a light on inside but no sign of anyone being about. I knocked at the back door; still no answer. I tried the handle; the door was unlocked and easily swung open at my touch. I stuck my head inside and shouted 'Hello!' There was no answer. I took a few tentative steps inside, still wearing my boots and rucksack, and shouted hello again. The place was deserted apart from a small black cat which sat in the middle of the hall staring at me with a knowing look on its face.

I try not to make a habit of entering a stranger's house alone and unannounced. It all felt a bit unnerving. I felt as if I was violating some trust, entering where I was not supposed to be, looking at their things when I hadn't been invited, a reluctant invader in a foreigner's country. I'd never make a burglar. I half expected the owner to leap out from some hidden place, irate and demanding to know who I was and what I was doing in their house, tramping my dirty boots across the carpet, and no, it wasn't the bed and breakfast and I could make my excuses to the local constabulary, who had already been summoned and were on their way with sirens blaring and blue lights flashing.

None of these things happened. On a side table, under a bronze paperweight shaped like a horse's head, were three sheets of paper. I picked them up and shuffled through them; one had my name on. The note informed me that they'd popped out for a bit and I was to go to room five and make myself comfortable.

The house was a shrine to foxhunting and horses. I climbed a set of stairs hung with riding crops and dressage top hats. Room five was along a corridor lined with gymkhana rosettes, hunting prints and photographs of the sort of ponies Thelwell made his name drawing. My room would have suited a Regency buck. There was a four-poster bed hung with faded green satin curtains, a broken Chippendale chair, an ancient-looking shower in one corner and a crystal chandelier draped with cobwebs. In the loo, along the corridor, there was a framed newspaper cutting announcing that Crown Prince Willem-Alexander, heir to the Dutch throne, had stayed there in 1998.

Most B&B owners are friendly, outgoing people who take an interest in their visitors; here there seemed to be a policy of minimal contact with the guests. I never did get to meet the lady of the house, she was always busy with the horses.

I escaped to the pub as soon as I could but that was a cheerless place too. Every table seemed to be full of couples engrossed with each other and when I went to the bar the landlord made it clear that he didn't want to chat. Craving some kind of contact after what had been a barren sort of a day I'd made my way home from the pub. Back at the B&B the small black cat was sitting on the side table where I'd found my 'welcome' note. I went over to make a fuss of her but she just looked at me with a pair of huge opal eyes then she lifted her furry bottom off the table, turned her back on me and farted.

The Gold Cup

Brimpsfield was a bit off route. So far off route, in fact, that it wasn't on my Cotswold Way map and I'd had to borrow a road atlas and draw myself a little sketch map to pick my way through the jumble of backroads to be able to find it. But I counted myself lucky just for having found somewhere to stay the night before the Cheltenham Gold Cup. Doubly lucky, as it turned out, because it was a B&B which didn't take in race goers, only Cotswold Way walkers.

There was no pub in Brimpsfield so the owners gave me a lift to the next village, where there was a pub, the Golden Hart, which had a reputation for good food. It's astounding sometimes the way some B&B owners will put themselves out for their guests. The pub was heaving with people who had all spent the day at the races and the talk was of horses, jockeys, photo finishes and who had won or lost. There was a noisy group at the next table. Four men, sharply dressed in city suits, brightly-coloured shirts and flashy cufflinks, were sitting around a table listening to a plump, blonde girl in pair of tight jodhpurs. She was called Fiona, and she was telling them all about her ex-boyfriend.

'Yeah it's all a bit boring really. So he dumped me and then got engaged to Rachel, so he doesn't go out much now. He has lots of sex but doesn't get out much.'

Next morning was Friday 13th, and Cheltenham Gold

Cup Day. It was raining when I set off to walk the mile and a half to Birdlip, where I would be back on my map. The rain had stopped but the clouds were low and there wasn't much to see from Barrow Wake View Point. Instead I watched a National Trust warden feeding a group of eight belted Galloway cattle. Their coats were misted by the rain, which softened their outline against the trees. They would have merged into the surrounding heath but for the broad shaggy white band around their middles. As the warden walked back to his Land Rover carrying the empty feed bucket one of the cows walked slowly up to him. He stroked her muzzle gently as if she were a pet and she turned around and followed him for a few steps and then she stopped and gazed blankly into the mist.

There was a long white stretch limo with dark tinted windows in the car park of the Air Balloon pub and the sound of laughter and clinking glasses was coming from inside. The traffic was nose to tail heading for the races along the A417, but once that obstacle was behind me (find a miniscule gap in the traffic, then sprint and hope) I was into quiet back lanes over Wistley Hill and Dowdeswell Reservoir.

As the weather improved the sky started to fill with helicopters as the well heeled and the well connected, who could afford to bypass the hold-ups at the Air Balloon Roundabout, went racing. In my own way small way I also 'went to the races'. I arrived on the top of Cleeve Hill, the highest point of the Cotswold Way, in time for the start of the big race and found myself a grassy spot just below the summit where I could look out over the elongated oval of the racetrack two miles away.

The afternoon sun reflected from the windscreens of ranks and ranks of parked cars and the stands were a shifting grey mass of people. Floating a hundred feet above the track and tethered to the ground by long guy ropes was a dirty-looking yellow barrage balloon, presumably to stop the helicopters taking a shortcut over the track and spooking the horses. Away to the right a field had been pressed into service as a temporary heliport, but all the choppers were grounded for the duration of the race.

There were many times on the walk when I wished I'd packed a pair of binoculars but never more so than sitting on Cleeve Hill on Gold Cup Day. It was difficult to pick out specific details but I could hear the sound of the public address system, tinny and indistinct, drifting across on the breeze, then the unmistakable words: 'They're off!' The PA settled into a monotonous rhythm, like an incantation, over the background rumble of the crowd. As the race progressed the tempo began to increase until the commentary became a high-pitched chant, like a Tibetan monk on speed, ramping up the excitement. Hooves were pounding the turf down there, fortunes were being staked, millions won and lost. The commentary became even faster, impossibly fast. How could anyone talk so fast? It rose to become a high-pitched babble, words indistinct, a banshee, demented, tormented. Then it stopped, suddenly and abruptly. For a second, Cleeve Hill was silent. Even the birds had stopped their singing. Then the roar started. It grew from nothing and swelled, it expanded and filled the air until it was the sound of thunder, a deep booming of bass drums reaching a crescendo, a hurricane rushing and roaring, filling the valley with noise and rolling over the hills. I've heard the expression 'a wall of sound'. This sound was tangible, like a physical thing. Like a wave breaking over Cleeve Hill it surrounded me, engulfed me, gripped me by the shoulders and held me there, inescapable, pressing in on me from every side. Then it loosened its grip, faded and subsided like the tide until it was something soft, a murmur, like a sigh and the birds in the bushes shook their feathers and resumed their singing. Ruby Walsh had just won the Cheltenham Gold Cup at seven to four on Kauto Star.

The bar and restaurant were heaving when I went down. There were people singing, there were people dancing, and a band, with two fiddlers, a banjo player and a drummer, were beating the life out of some Irish tunes. It seemed to me that what the people at the bar were singing bore no resemblance to what the band was playing but nobody seemed particularly worried about this. It was boozy, boisterous, noisy and good-natured. It was Christmas night, New Year's Eve, St Patrick's Day and the end of term party all rolled into one.

When I tried to get to the dining room, a short man wearing a black fedora and an overcoat which went down almost to his ankles caught hold of me and waltzed me twice around the dance floor before I could escape and go in for something to eat.

At the next table a group of a dozen race goers, celebrating their win, launched into a chorus of 'Delaney's Donkey'. The manager rushed across and shouted over the din, 'If you carry on like that you'll have to leave.'

When I next looked across he had his arms around their shoulders, his head back and they were all singing 'Rosemary'.

After five days of solitary walking the atmosphere was compelling, welcoming and warm. After my meal I lingered, sitting at the back watching the dancers stagger around the floor, and listening to beer soaked renditions of songs that I had forgotten or had never learnt. I might have only watched the race from the top of Cleeve Hill and

I might know less than nothing about horses or horse racing but for that night, I was one of them.

I had a bit of a sore head next morning.

Dover's Hill and the Olympics

The hotel on Cleeve Hill had a back gate which opened straight out onto the golf course and the Cotswold Way. I was a bit slow off the mark and still feeling a tad fragile after the previous night's end-of-Cheltenham festivities.

It seems to me that footpaths and golf courses share an uneasy relationship. Golf clubs don't really like walkers in rucksacks and boots tramping across their fairways but if that's where the footpath goes then they really can't do very much about it. Footpaths across golf courses tend to start out as well-marked tracks but fade away to nothing somewhere around the fourth tee or they get confused with the golfers' paths, and if a walker unintentionally drifts off route it can lead to unpleasant confrontations with chaps who have singular tastes in woolly jumpers and a penchant for chequered Rupert Bear trousers. Also, and perhaps more to the point, walkers never get invited back to the nineteenth hole.

It was almost ten o'clock when I set out across the course and as it was Saturday the tees were already busy with golfers. It was clear something was wrong right from the off. The path signposted 'Cotswold Way' wasn't heading in the same direction as the one marked on my map. I made an initial foray down the track hoping it might take a late swerve back to the proper route but no, it kept resolutely heading in the wrong direction. I backtracked to where I had started and studied the map closely, trying to ignore the watching eyes of the golfers still waiting at the tee, smirking and nudging each other. It's not that I mind getting lost. I've long been a follower of the great G.H.B. Ward, leader of the Sheffield Clarion Ramblers in the 1920s and 30s, who famously stated: 'The man who was never lost, never went very far.' It's just that if I do get lost, I'd rather not have an audience. And if I have to have an audience, I'd rather that audience wasn't made up of Saturday morning golfers.

But there was really no alternative. The route marked on my map lined up exactly with the trajectory that the golfers, the more accurate ones anyway, were whacking their golf balls. So I had to follow the path I'd tried in the first place and hope that it was right and my map was wrong.

The path ran away from the tee, the bunkers and low flying golf balls, skirted around the edge of the course and dropped down through a wood and past Postlip Hall. It was evident by this point that for once it wasn't down to my map reading, the route really was different. In fact the route was better, since the one marked on my map dipped south for a mile or so before swinging back to the north again and heading south for any sort of distance goes against the grain when the ultimate goal is John O'Groats.

I had been impressed with the Cotswolds and the Cotswold Way. Apart from the confusion across the golf course, the route was well planned and so well marked the map was almost superfluous. If a walker follows the signs they shouldn't really get lost (I did of course, but I really had to work at it). The Cotswold people I spoke to along the way seemed proud of their long distance footpath and seemed to take it as something of a compliment when people came along and walked it. Also I had been very lucky with the weather. After the snow squall in Bath and a bit of drizzle at Birdlip the weather had been good and it was noticeable how the ground had dried out and became less muddy as the walk progressed. I was only sorry that I was walking it so early in the spring before the leaves had started to grow on the trees and made myself a mental note to come back again sometime after the trees had greened up.

After most of the walk being so welcoming it came as a bit of a jolt, on a path down towards Winchcombe, to pass through an area which clearly wasn't so walker-friendly. It's not hard to tell when a landowner doesn't really want walkers. Signs appear fixed to gates and fences: 'Private, Keep to Footpath', and 'Dogs on Lead' and a little further along, 'Keep Strictly to Footpaths'. If they were hoping to discourage walkers it wasn't working. It was the weekend, the sun was shining and after hardly meeting a walker on the trail so far there were hikers and ramblers everywhere.

The village of Broadway, with its wide main street and houses built from honey-coloured Cotswold stone, looked as if it had decked itself out with early spring flowers specially for the visitors. It was a little too busy for me to want to linger so I pressed on to Broadway Tower at the top of the hill and then over to Fish Hill, where I started to notice how the accents of the people I talked to along the way had started to change from a West Country lilt to more of a Midlands drawl.

I had almost completed the Cotswold Way. I just had Dover's Hill to go. From the viewpoint there I could still see across to the River Severn to the hills of Wales, which felt like a bit of a let down. I know the Bristol Channel and then the River Severn run for a long way inland but I had rather hoped that I'd shaken them off by this time. I had been looking out over them since Selwothy Beacon, which was before Minehead, and they were still out there, stalking me. But I had a trick or two up my sleeve: I'd head for Birmingham and give them the slip.

Dover's Hill, the last hill of the Cotswold Way, has another, and rather unique, claim to fame. Since 1636 it has been the site of Robert Dover's Cotswold Olympic Games. These were proper games, not like those softy Greek ones. Proper games and proper sports, Cotswold sports where they roll up their trouser legs and go in for a bout of shin-kicking or pike tumbling.

I walked down Dover's Hill and into Chipping Campden with mixed feelings. There was a warm feeling of satisfaction at having completed the Cotswold Way, which was what I'd set out to do. But the same sense of sadness I felt at the end of the South West Coast Path, the feeling that it was the end of a section of the walk which I'd enjoyed so much and moving on was like saying goodbye to a friend. I was also beginning to doubt the wisdom of my choice of route for the next stage of the walk.

My idea of walking through Britain was that I should experience the changes of landscape as I progressed: the highs, the lows, the scenic and the not so scenic. Which was fine and all very laudable at the planning stage and while I was strolling through areas of outstanding natural beauty but less so when confronted by a hike through the Black Country. Depending upon how you define industrial, there are two industrial belts which form obstacles to a broadly green route from Land's End to John O'Groats: the Midlands and southern Scotland, around Edinburgh and Glasgow. How you navigate your way through these areas will have a big impact on the walk overall. One trick is to avoid the Midlands altogether. To swing out west beyond Bristol, head for Wales then work your way north along the Welsh border and Offa's Dyke. But this requires a massive detour out west, and later another big detour back east again through Staffordshire. I, on the other hand, was planning to follow a more or less a central line up through the contrasting environments of the Midlands until I reached Edale at the foot of the Pennine Way. It may be a journey through our industrial heritage but I was worried about the very real prospect of no decent walking country until I reached Derbyshire and the Peak District.

But for now, at least my hangover had cleared so perhaps a modest celebration for walking the Cotswold Way would be in order.

The Bones of the Bard

I left Chipping Campden heading for Stratford-upon-Avon, the home of the Bard. The route north took me down a quiet side road, through a stand of trees which marked the line of the Campden Tunnel, then past the National Trust's Hidcote Manor to join Cycle Route 5 through to Stratford.

I made a halt at Lower Quinton, where I sat on a bench beside the village green to have a late morning cup of coffee out of my thermos flask. Approaching Lower Quinton from the south it seemed like the quintessential English village. There was an attractive church with a neat spire and a war memorial in the churchyard. A welcoming pub faced out across the village green and there was a duck pond with a group of noisy ducks who waddled over to scrounge a few crumbs from my elevenses. The May blossom was just coming into bloom and there was a row of tidy cottages, some with thatched roofs. There was even a cheerful, and rather rotund, post lady who came wobbling along on a push bike with letters, parcels and packages stuffed into a basket fixed to the handlebars. If Agatha Christie had been stuck for somewhere for Miss Marple to live, and she hadn't invented St Mary-Mead, she could have done a lot worse than to set her lady sleuth in Lower Quinton.

The northern end of the village was a bit of a let down by comparison. There were signs saying 'STOP ECO NEW TOWN' and the village became an urban sprawl of modern and rather featureless houses. Beyond the village was a mile or two of semi industrial land with railway tracks and warehouses, some of which looked big enough to hide a couple of jumbo jets but, judging by the activity I could see through the fence, it looked as if it was a depot for car importers.

Just before Long Marston the cycle route swung right to run along the Greenway, a disused railway line leading to Stratford. I always had mixed feelings about walking these tracks along disused railway lines. At first sight they seem heaven-sent for the long distance walker – they are flat, even and generally have a good surface to walk on – and I always start out on these tracks with a surge of energy and enthusiasm and quickly begin to make good progress. But somewhere around the two mile mark the monotony starts to kick in, the sameness of all these tracks, the lack of features and landmarks, it all starts to become boring, tedious and energy sapping. Perverse creatures these long distance walkers, we grumble at rough ground, we moan about the hills and go into a positive sulk when we get stuck in a bog, but give us a smooth section of easy to follow, flat, disused railway line and still we're not happy.

As the afternoon wore on I started to meet joggers and dog walkers coming in the other direction, a sure sign I was coming to a town. I walked passed Stratford Race Course (you don't pass a racetrack for miles then two come along, one after the other) and just beyond I was tempted to take the path along the River Avon but decided to stick to my old friend Cycle Route 5 (I was beginning to feel that we were joined at the hip by this time). It proved to be a good move as it took me right past my B&B so I was able to dump my pack there and walk into town unencumbered.

I have a soft spot for Stratford-upon-Avon. After never having done any Shakespeare at school I 'discovered' him in my mid-thirties and have been hooked ever since. So taken was I that when it came to getting married, Stratford-upon-Avon was the place we chose to tie the knot. There were, of course, practical reasons. My wife's family came from the south, and mine from the north, so we decided we would get married somewhere in between. We spread out the map, closed our eyes, jabbed a pin into it and the pin stuck in Stratford-upon-Avon. Actually it stuck in Sutton Coldfield first but we moved it to Stratford pretty damn quick.

I wandered into town feeling a stone lighter, having shed my pack, and took a stroll past Shakespeare's Birthplace, then past the theatre and on into the park and sat by his memorial with it's statues of Hamlet, Prince Hal, Falstaff and Lady Macbeth. It occurred to me as I sat there that I'd never visited the Bard's grave so, on impulse, I decided to go to Holy Trinity Church to put this right. I was lucky, a service had just finished as I arrived, so I was able to go in and see where he had been buried in the chancel, not far from the altar. His wife, Anne Hathaway, and other members of his family were buried beside him and there is a not very flattering bust of the great man fixed to the wall. Surprisingly Shakespeare's name does not appear on his grave, instead there is a curious, and now very famous, inscription.

Good friend, for Jesus' sake forbeare,
To dig the dust encloased heare.
Bleste be the man that spares thes stones
And curst be he that moves my bones.

There have been initiatives, over the years, to dig up his remains and re-inter them in Poets' Corner at Westminster Abbey. I, for one, am glad they haven't and I wouldn't like to be the man who moved his bones.

On the way out a lady priest, still wearing her green embroidered vestments and stole from having just taken the service, stopped me and asked me if I'd come far.

'I've walked here from Bath,' I said. The way it came out sounded rather more smug than I'd intended.

'From Bath?' she said. A perplexed look crossed her face. 'But why walk all the way from Bath?'

'Well ...' suddenly I was tongue-tied. How could I answer that without going into the whole story of redundancy and retirement and vain attempts to hold back my ever-advancing years. 'You see I retired last year and ... well I've never seen Shakespeare's tomb and ...' I tailed off.

'Oh a sort of a pilgrimage? But why from Bath?'

'Well no not a pilgrimage as such. More of a walk and ...' It still felt too early to confess to anyone, even a priest, that I was walking Land's End to John O'Groats, far too many miles to go and still far too much like tempting fate.

Seeing how stuck for words I was she just smiled and told me that I was welcome at Holy Trinity Church and walked away towards the sanctuary. Why couldn't I put it into words? I'd never thought of my walk as a pilgrimage before but I suppose in one sense I was definitely seeking something. But what? My lost youth? It was a bit late for that. Some sort of meaning perhaps, a sense of purpose in life, now that I was superfluous to requirements, at least as far as the world of work was concerned? Well maybe. No sense in dwelling on the matter, I thought, I'd just have to get on with the job, my new job that is, the job of moving my own old bones, and in the general direction of John O'Groats.

The Forest of Arden

As I was in Stratford-upon-Avon it seemed a shame to leave without going to the theatre. The old Shakespeare Theatre on the banks of the River Avon was undergoing a major refit, hidden under a mountain of scaffolding and topped by a couple of massive cranes, but it was business as usual at the Courtyard and I was able to get in to see a production of *As You Like It*. This couldn't have been more appropriate because the bulk of the action takes place in the Forest of Arden, which was where the next day's walk would take me.

Orlando, the hero of the play, joins a bunch of outlaws and hides out with them, deep in the forest, after defeating Charles, Duke Frederick's wrestler. He woos the fair Rosalind, who, in typical Shakespearean fashion, has also run away into the forest disguised as a man and calling herself Ganymede. There the story unfolds with a motley bunch of characters including Touchstone, a jester, and a rather morose individual called Jaques who makes the famous 'Seven Ages of Man' speech.

On my way back from the theatre I found myself pondering just where I'd fit in Shakespeare's seven ages of man? Jaques tended to fudge the issue when it came to redundancy or early retirement. I didn't think I was quite in the seventh age yet, the old man who is generally past it: 'Sans teeth, sans eyes, sans taste, sans everything.' So working backwards there was the sixth age: 'the lean and slippered pantaloons. With spectacles on nose ... shrunk shank ... big, manly voice, turning again toward childish treble.' Well there were spectacles perched on my nose but they'd been there since I was fourteen. I'd never had a big manly voice, and since I'd been on the walk my shanks, if anything, had grown bigger instead of shrinking. That left the fifth age: 'In fair round belly, with good capon lined.

With eyes severe, and beard of formal cut. Full of wise saws and modern instances'. That sounded a bit more like it, and at least you get to have a hearty meal, and I'd be needing all the hearty meals I could get before I took my 'fair round belly ... eyes severe and beard of formal cut' off, like Orlando, Jaques, Ganymede and the rest of the crew, into the Forest of Arden.

'Nutter!' yelled the slack-jawed youth at me out of the side window of his Ford Fiesta. The traffic lights had changed a bit quicker than I'd bargained for and I'd rather spoilt his wheel-spinning, rubber-burning power start. Nothing sets up the day, for the recently retired walker, than upsetting a motorist on his way to work.

I was back following my old friend Cycle Route 5 and was quickly away from the rust-pocked Ford Fiestas and the rest of the traffic and onto the quiet banks of the Stratford Canal. I followed this as far as Wilmcote then continued on a backroad past Mary Arden's House.

In truth I couldn't find much evidence of where the Forest of Arden used to be. There were trees, but most were in the front gardens of smart houses, and instead of being the mighty oaks and ashes, to which Orlando had nailed his love notes to Rosalind, they were neatly-pruned flowering cherries all shedding pink blossoms in the breeze which was blowing them down the road like confetti after a wedding. Jaques and Touchstone would be weeping into their flagons of ale. The only clue that this once was a forest came just before Coughton. I had walked through Great Alne and crossed the River Arrow when I found, alongside the busy A435, a monument which looked as if it could once have been the base of a stone cross. And it was there, according to the inscription, that travellers would stop and pray for safe passage through the Forest of Arden.

The country had flattened out considerably since the Cotswolds. It was an area of quiet lanes, pasture land and isolated woods with bluebells beginning to push their way up through what was left of the leaf litter. I took a break, and sat on the village green at Sambourne. It was a warm afternoon and I even dozed a bit. I wanted to savour this last bit of green and pleasant countryside because this was where it ended. I didn't have to go far before I was into towns and the built-up areas around Studley and Redditch.

As part of the on-going battle to keep down the weight I was carrying I had ditched my usual Ordnance Survey Landranger maps and, as I'd mostly been following cycle routes, I was navigating by a small-scale cycle route map. These are great maps if you are on a bike or following a cycle path but they are not designed for route finding away from cycle paths, where the detail starts to become a bit more sketchy. My problem, that afternoon, was that Cycle Route 5 swung to the east of Redditch and I needed to head around to the west to find the pub where I was supposed to be staying in a part of town known as Headless Cross. I learnt very quickly that Redditch is impregnable to anyone approaching on foot. It doesn't need turrets, castles or city walls, it is more than adequately protected by rank upon rank of bypasses, roundabouts, industrial parks and urban wastelands, none of which were identifiable from my map.

I'd learnt a valuable lesson back in Somerset when I struggled to find Street Youth Hostel. So I'd started typing the postcode of the place I was due to stay into one of the street-map websites and printing off a small local map. These maps had a very helpful big yellow arrow pointing to the exact place I was trying to find. This is just what every End to Ender dreams about: a big yellow arrow telling them exactly where to go. It made my life a whole lot easier and saved me hours of futile tramping around towns and villages. I'd done the same for Redditch but this was where I discovered that this system, like every other system, wasn't entirely foolproof. I couldn't square up the roads on my cycle map or the roads on my internet-print-off map, with the apparently random arrangement of bypasses, trunk roads and junctions on the outskirts of town. And the big yellow arrow was no flipping help either. It wasn't a walker-friendly place and I had the feeling that I really shouldn't be there at all. The only plus was that the roads had wide grass verges so I could keep well back from the traffic which was thundering past beside me without a break. In desperation I had to resort to the trial and error method. This is not, incidentally, a technique recommended by any of the more reputable Land's End to John O'Groats books. I would follow a road which was heading in, what I hoped, was the right direction. I'd follow it for a for a mile or so until I saw something, some distinctive feature, a landmark, anything, which I could equate with either of my maps or which might give me the slightest indication of where the hell I was. If I found nothing after, say, a couple of miles, I'd backtrack and try another road. What I needed to find, at least according to the big yellow arrow, was the junction of Coldfield Drive and the A448.

I think I was following my third trial and error route when I saw a slip road with a signpost for Headless Cross. Yippee! I followed it. About half a mile later I found the road junction I thought I was looking for. My, now much-thumbed and rather dog-eared, dot-com street map showed it as a regular road junction. It was not. I was standing at sub-ground level by the A448 while the traffic trundled along Coldfield Drive at least fifty feet above my head. Most of the End to End books frankly duck the issue when it comes to how you deal with overpasses, underpasses and flyovers. It was getting late in the day and I was getting desperate. Drastic situations call for drastic actions and anyway there was nothing else I could do. I took a quick look in both directions, to check for any approaching prowl cars, and then took a run at the embankment. Fuelled by a heady mix of adrenaline and fear I scrambled up the bank, bringing feet, knees, elbows and hands all into play, and ... I made it, just. I grabbed hold of the metal fencing at the top, wild-eyed, sweating and gasping for breath. I'm afraid I must have given the three elderly ladies who were waiting at the bus stop up there quite a nasty shock when I appeared, apparently from nowhere, shinned over the fence, bid them 'Good afternoon' and walked away whistling nonchalantly. So this was Headless Cross. More like Headless Chicken.

One Third
I didn't fare much better finding my way out of Redditch next morning. Redditch is a place which has suffered from a very bad case of town planners. No doubt, a few years back, the City Fathers decided that the old parts of town needed ripping out and that new modern roads and people-friendly walkways should be built instead. I left Headless Cross and tried to find my way to the town centre along a network of pleasant, leafy and landscaped pathways which snake their way through the suburbs. In most places the world over, a general rule of thumb applies: if you're not sure of the way and there is a footpath or a road heading in roughly the right direction and you follow it, nine times out of ten it will take you to the place where you want to be, or at least to somewhere very close to it. This rule does not apply in Redditch.

The paths (and they were very nice paths, all landscaped and tidy) started out hopefully enough but then they would swerve off in a graceful arc and end up going somewhere quite different. At one point I followed a path signposted for the 'Town Centre'. After ten minutes I stopped a passer-by to ask the way and she told me I was going in exactly the opposite direction to the centre of town.

It took me two hours to find my way out of Redditch, by which time I felt I was personally acquainted with every single footpath and walkway in town. I was also familiar with the B&Q, the Homebase, the sports centre and even the crematorium.

After Redditch I arrived on Icknield Street, or Ryknild Street as it was called on my map. I was back, and with some relief, on an Ordnance Survey map by this time. Icknield Street is a ramrod-straight Roman road, which I followed due north for five miles. It quickly became a narrow lane set in a slight hollow between the fields and ran under the M42 motorway and past a small circular pond where the dozen or so men fishing were so still they could have been carved from stone.

It was the top spot locally for burning out stolen cars. I passed two charred wrecks and a pull-in where the tarmac had been melted and all the trees scorched. Under my boots, as I walked along, I crunched shards of windscreen, broken headlight bulbs and other small but unidentifiable remnants of the automotive industry.

I left Icknield Street where it swung away to the right and continued over Primrose Hill, past the cemetery and down into a housing estate. At King's Norton I joined the canal towpath and was back on my old friend Cycle Route 5 again, all the way into Birmingham.

I had tried every way I could, at the planning stage of

the walk, to choose a route which avoided Birmingham. When I was a teenager I remember riding on a bus out of Birmingham and going to Warwick. I think it was Warwick, or it might have been Stratford-upon-Avon. It was the most tedious, monotonous and seemingly endless bus ride ever. It went for miles and miles through featureless, dull and unremarkable suburbs and the prospect of walking through these same streets to get into and out of the city did not appeal. And, based on my recent experiences in Redditch, I thought I would be in for a grim afternoon. But just as all roads lead to Rome, all canals lead to Birmingham, so I'd just have to grit my teeth, gird up my rucksack and get on with it. I couldn't have been more wrong.

I started along the canal at King's Norton and then followed the River Rea Trail, which made a green corridor right into the heart of the city. I went through Hazelwell Park and then on to Cannon Hill Park. These are proper parks, just like the parks I can remember from when I was a kid. Cannon Hill Park has a boating lake, tennis courts and, on the day I passed through, lots and lots of spotty teenagers dossing around and snogging on the grass. There were kids playing on the swings, bigger kids kicking footballs about and babies being pushed along in prams by proud mothers. There was even a pavilion where they sold ice cream, buns and cups of tea.

From the park it was just a short hop, via Edgbaston Cricket Ground, to the city centre. Even this was a revelation. I don't think I'd ever been any further than the Bullring before, I certainly hadn't been to Victoria Square with its grand buildings and imposing statues. I loved the simplicity of Antony Gormley's *Iron:Man* and what red-blooded man could fail to be enticed by the voluptuous charms of *The Floozie in the Jacuzzi*? Even if on that day some mean-hearted soul had drained all the water out of the poor girl's Jacuzzi.

And as if these heady delights were not enough, my little orange map-measuring friend informed me I'd walked 418 miles and that was a third of the way to John O'Groats.

Next morning I joined the canal again opposite the National Sea Life Centre, by the smart and newly regenerated marina. Birmingham is said to have more canals than Venice (but rather fewer gondoliers) and this was one of the main canal junctions. There was even a traffic roundabout for barges. It was a bit like stepping back in time, a tour through the industrial heritage of the Midlands. Even a photographer taking pictures of the narrow boats seemed to be in period. He had an old-fashioned large format camera on a wooden tripod with a black cloth which he draped over his head when he looked through the lens to focus.

The towpath led out of the city through Ladywood and Winson Green. Factories crowded on each bank, from some there came the sound of hammering and crashing, others lay silent and derelict, their corrugated iron walls a rusty canvas for graffiti artists. Every quarter of a mile or so a road bridge would cross the canal high above, so high it was impossible to see the traffic from the towpath below. The cars, buses and lorries on the road all belonged to another world, the modern world, the world of the twenty-first century, whilst below, down by the canal, it was part of an earlier and a slower era. The canal was a link to the past, a ribbon of smooth water, the home to swans and moorhens. A world only shared with the occasional narrow boat, a cyclist or two, a solitary End to End walker and a fisherman whose eyes never moved from a tiny red float a few feet from the tip of his rod.

The map showed the cycle route as criss-crossing the

canal two or three times while, on the ground, it was clear that it remained on the right-hand bank all the way. There was a set of confusing signs around the Smethwick Junction, where the canal seemed to split into two and the route followed the right bank of the left-hand canal. The map wasn't much help really and I was beginning to take the route marked on it with a pinch of salt and to follow what seemed the logical route on the ground. I would come to regret this strategy a bit later in the day.

By late morning I left the canal via a ramp just beyond the Galton Tunnel and worked my way past lorry depots and through some grim roads, under the M5 motorway and on to West Bromwich. Previously on the walk, crossing a motorway was always something of a landmark, a tick-off feature on the map which would confirm my exact position. But around Birmingham the motorways came thick and fast. I was going over and under so many of them I had quite lost track of which motorway was which.

I did know that it was the M5 which ran alongside the path by Sandwell Park for a short but noisy spell and I was grateful to turn aside past Swan Pool, where there were yet more fishermen. The Swan Pool anglers clearly took their business very seriously. They were set up as if for laying siege with tents, sleeping bags and camping stoves. The nearest angler climbed, dishevelled and unshaven, out of his tent and scowled at me. Then he turned his back and started to grub around in a blue plastic bucket and make up balls of crumbly-looking brown stuff, ground bait I suppose, which he loaded one ball at a time into a sort of throwing stick and then he hurled them as far out into the lake as he could. They landed in the water with a loud splash. After each throw he would turn around to glare at me. Perhaps he was close to perfecting a new and deadly ground bait, irresistible to all fish. Perhaps he suspected me of being engaged in a little piscatorial espionage on behalf of some rival fishing club. Either way, I had the distinct feeling that if I stayed there watching any longer he would start throwing the balls of ground bait at me so I took the hint and left him to it. Fisherman don't enjoy being watched, unless of course they are actually catching fish.

I pressed on, across the River Tame, to Forge Mill Lake and Sandwell Bird Reserve. I have been known to indulge in a bit of birdwatching on occasion and I knew that Sandwell Bird Reserve was run by the Royal Society for the Protection of Birds. The RSPB is a well set-up organisation and I knew from experience that a bird reserve means a visitor centre, and a visitor centre means a café and a café means cups of tea. I'd walked from Birmingham without a break and at that moment would have killed for a cup of tea. I found a sign which read 'Visitor Centre 1,000 metres'. That was 1,000 metres (what – about two thirds of a mile?) off my route and then another 1,000 metres back again. Then there was the question of whether the visitor centre would actually have a café, and if it did would the café be open? Was it worth the risk and was it worth the detour? I thought how delicious a cup of tea and a slice of flapjack would be, and then I thought of what I had by way of comestibles in my backpack: a bottle of tap water and the crumbling remains of a packet of Hobnobs. I decided to risk it, all 1,000 metres of it. The walk there might be a bit of a drag but the 1,000 metres back would seem like nothing at all, not when I was fuelled with tea and cake.

It was level walking on a good path through open scrubland, with the occasional sidetrack leading off to a bird viewing hide. I didn't see many birds but I saw lots of bird watchers with binoculars slung around their necks and carrying professional-looking telescopes fixed to

102

tripods. The visitor centre stood in the middle of a small clearing. There was a sign outside, a sort of whiteboard, listing the birds which had been seen that morning and another smaller sign next to it with the magic words 'Hot Drinks' excellent, and a picture on the sign of a steaming mug of coffee. Better and better, my cup runneth over. Inside the visitor centre there wasn't a café as such but there was a vending machine. Okay well that's better than nothing, I thought. And taped to the vending machine, handwritten in green marker pen was a notice which read, 'Out of Order, sorry for the inconvenience'. Oh ... never has 1,000 metres felt longer, tedious or more foot-draggingly depressing than the 1,000 metres back through the bird reserve all the way back to rejoin my proper route. Bugger.

On a Compass Bearing to Walsall

As soon as I was back on my proper route, I got lost. The Midlands was rapidly becoming a catalogue of me going adrift but this was the worst 'got lost' of the whole walk so far. I'd taken the wrong path before, I'd gone down the wrong road before, but this was the first time I'd ever followed the wrong canal. If I'm honest I'd started to become just a little bit blasé about Cycle Route 5. I'd come to regard it as a sort of general guide rather than something I should follow in an exact way as per the map. There may have been a crucial signpost missing, I can't be sure, and I didn't go back to find out. Or I might, in my tea-starved state, just not have been taking enough notice of where I was going and what I was doing. So instead of walking for a short stretch along the Rushall Canal and then turning off for Yew Tree and working my way through the lanes to Walsall, I found I was on a canal, which I was pretty sure wasn't the Rushall, with not a hint of a turn-off and hard up against the nose-to-tail traffic of the adjacent motorway. And I wasn't even sure which motorway it was.

Getting lost also seemed to coincide with a subtle change in the mood. Instead of the canalside feeling a welcoming and homely place, like it did back in Birmingham, it started to feel an alien environment where the landmarks on the ground resolutely refused to match up with anything on my map. Even the other canal users had ceased to be the friendly and cheery types I'd been meeting all morning. They had become sinister, suspicious and hostile. Two fishermen sitting on the far bank cast me baleful glances and wouldn't return my greeting. A bunch of teenage lads riding bikes, which looked far too small for them, came bombing down the towpath, driving me into the long grass. As they sped past one of them, a tow-haired youth with yellowed, uneven teeth, shouted something abusive but quite unintelligible at me.

Apart from going forward or back there wasn't any way, short of swimming, to get off the towpath. The oily, dark waters of the canal were on one side, the busy motorway on the other, and there were no bridges. I pressed on beside this stinking cut, with its abandoned supermarket trolleys, fleets of rusty cans and old pop bottles floating on the surface for a mile or two, then, the first chance I got, I escaped. I came alongside a muddy bank, which I scrambled up on all fours, dodging a couple of rusting washing machines and several piles of dog turds. I climbed over a barbed wire fence at the top and came out onto a busy road. I wasn't sure where I was escaping to but it had to be better than being down by the canal.

I found myself on a main road with lorries and buses going past. I was in luck. I was due a bit of luck. I had come out on Walsall Road and Walsall was, after all, my next port of call. But my map didn't have road names marked so I still couldn't plot exactly where I was. But if I was on Walsall Road it was a pretty fair bet that if I followed it then eventually it would lead me to Walsall itself. All I needed was to decide whether I went to the left or the right. My gut feeling said go right, but my gut feeling had just got me lost. It's not often you see someone dressed in all their walking gear standing next to a bus shelter on a busy road in the outskirts of Walsall taking a compass bearing, but that's exactly what I did. I may have felt just a tad foolish but if I hadn't taken that compass bearing, and I had followed my gut feeling to go right, I would have finished up back in West Bromwich. So I set off walking to the left and after a few minutes I passed a railway station, Tame Bridge Parkway Station, and that *was* marked on my map. At last all the landmarks, after having had an afternoon of freedom, reluctantly gave up their game of hide-and-seek and started to fall back into their allotted places as per the map, and I went off to find my hotel, which, as it turned out, was nearly as big a mistake as spending the afternoon getting lost.

The hotel, which I'd booked over the internet, was so close to the M6 as to be almost under the flyover. I should have guessed what it would be like when it was so cheap. It catered mostly for workmen renovating the houses nearby. The dress code was quite formal, only overalls, hard hats and brick dust would do. Ronnie, a plasterer from Tyne and Wear, told me the hotel was popular with the lads because they charged less per night than the contractor gave them for their subsistence. The excess almost covered their beer and fag money.

The carpet in my room was so grubby I kept my boots on and there were bare wires sticking out of the wall. In the bathroom, when I turned on the shower, the sprinkler flew off and sent a jet of water up the wall and this then ran down and soaked the loo roll. Next morning at breakfast, a woman in a ketchup-stained apron reminded me that I still had to pay for a couple of drinks on my tab from the previous night before she ran through a list of things which they hadn't got for breakfast. The list included bacon, sausages and cornflakes. At least I wasn't tempted to linger. I was soon on my way and off to explore the town.

Walsall's claim to fame is making the finest harnesses and saddles for horses. Even Walsall Football Club, whose ground, the Bescot Stadium, I'd passed by shortly after my life-saving compass bearing, is nicknamed 'The Saddlers'.

The sign for Cycle Route 5 pointed straight into the Town Council Offices but even I, with my recent track record for misnavigation, wasn't going to fall for that one. Local lads think it's a hoot to point signs in the opposite direction. I wondered how many cyclists they got riding up the steps in their helmets and Lycra, sitting astride their bikes looking around confused and bewildered, amongst all the people queuing to pay their council tax. So works the fevered imagination of the End to End walker marooned in the Midlands.

The proper route out of town was via Mill Hill Nature Reserve, which was a valiant attempt by the authorities to try to make something out of a nearby open space and one which the local youths were doing their best to wreck with spray-painted graffiti and by burning down the signposts. For all that, as I made my way down through the wood I found myself face-to-face with a small red fox. This was the first fox I'd seen on the walk. He was standing in the middle of the path giving me a bit of a quizzical look. I stood very still. The fox cocked his head on one side and had a good look at me for about a minute then, deciding he'd seen enough, he trotted away and disappeared into the undergrowth.

Beyond Mill Hill was a stretch of open and deserted wasteland with houses backing on to it, then beyond Pelsall I walked a short wooded stretch of the Wryley and Essingham Canal before arriving at Brownhills.

If Brownhills doesn't convince the visitor that it is an ex-mining town then it isn't for want of trying. On a traffic roundabout, near the main street, stands a massive statue of a miner. He is constructed from what seems to be a patchwork of stainless steel plates riveted together. The miner has his pit helmet on his head and is holding a short pickaxe aloft in one hand and a safety lamp in the other. I've known a lot of miners and have even been down a mine once or twice but I've never seen a miner strike quite such a pose. It is reminiscent of the art of Communist and Eastern Bloc countries which depicts the worker-hero.

Brownhills marked the far edge of the industrial areas. I crossed under the M6 toll road, walked around Chasewater Reservoir, then it was leafy lanes all the way into Litchfield. I knew I was back in proper countryside when I spotted a small herd of deer at Burntwood Sports Village; they'd found their way onto the rugby pitch and were busy cropping the turf on the halfway line.

The Beer Capital of the World
It was raining when I set off from Lichfield but despite the weather I thought it was worth taking a quick tour around town. It was still early so I didn't get to see Samuel Johnson's birthplace and could only look at the cathedral from the outside, which was a shame because I would have liked to have gone in to see the Francis Chantry sculpture of *The Sleeping Children*. The ever-present need to cover

my allotted miles each day meant I just didn't have much time to linger. This was turning out to be an unforeseen drawback of the walk. I wasn't trying to break any End to End records but there was still a pressure to keep going, to put the miles in and there were things I missed seeing along the way. I added Lichfield, and its cathedral, to my growing list of places to come back to sometime and to visit again after the walk, next time at a little bit more of a leisurely pace.

There were two ponds on the way out of town, but my map had only one, Stowe Pool, marked. This caused me a bit of head scratching, backtracking and intense map studying. I'd come to hate looking at maps in the middle of town. Well-meaning people come up to you and ask if you know where you are or whether you are lost. At least the rain stopped while I was wandering around town. The morning's walk was a tedious affair following straight and seemingly endless lanes between hawthorn hedges and past, somewhere deep in the middle of nowhere, a massive Tesco depot.

When I reached the village of Alrewas I made a detour, an intentional one for a change. I took my life into my hands and crossed the busy A38 then went to visit the National Memorial Arboretum. Being a Saturday, and also ANZAC Day, it was busy as coaches arrived with parties of war veterans.

The National Memorial Arboretum was opened in 1997 and there was still a newly-landscaped look about the place. The main monument has been built on a small mound, and at its centre is a tall white monolith which looked something like, I imagine, Cleopatra's Needle would have looked centuries ago when it was new. Enclosing the monolith on two sides, curved like a pair of brackets, are walls lined with black steel sculptures, depicting scenes of war and casualties being carried out on stretchers. Dotted around the grounds amongst the immature trees are other smaller memorials to specific military campaigns or individual regiments, there was even some rubble from Ground Zero. Most of the visitors were old men in smartly-pressed blazers with their medals pinned proudly on the front and regimental berets on their heads. They walked along slowly and stiffly, leaning on walking sticks or on a friend's arm, and made their way from one memorial to another. Sometimes they stopped and gazed at the long lists of fallen soldiers, and then I would see them run a finger slowly down the lists, trying to find the name of an old comrade.

I had a quick cup of tea in the café amongst the veterans then pressed on to a place which I suspected most of the old soldiers would have heartily approved of: Burton upon Trent, the beer capital of the world.

Next morning I left town past Burton Albion FC's Pirelli Stadium and crossed into Derbyshire, where, a bit further along, I came across the village of Etwall. I'd never been to Etwall before but it was a place which had remained stuck fast in my memory because of a local controversy which had blown up in the late 1970s, not long after I had started nursing. Etwall had a small hospital which mostly catered for elderly patients and the Health Authority, in its infinite wisdom, at that time had a policy of closing all the small local hospitals and so Etwall Hospital was due for the axe. The NHS works in cycles. It will decide to shut all local hospitals and spend millions concentrating health services in big district general hospitals. Then a few years later, there will be a change of management and a change of thinking, and it will spend millions more building lots of small community hospitals all over the county and farming out services from the big district general hospitals to the new local ones. Etwall found itself caught up in one such cycle and despite a local outcry and all the usual petitions, banners and protests, Etwall Hospital was shut and the staff were transferred, some with considerable reluctance, to other hospitals including Kingsway Hospital in Derby where I was based for my nurse training.

A few weeks later I discovered something of the strength of feeling locally. The closing of Etwall Hospital more or less coincided with me having a spell of working nights. I was nominally left in charge one night on Monsal Ward, an old psycho-geriatric back-ward, when Auxiliary Nurse Bostock was assigned to be working the shift with me. Heady at the prospect of being left in charge for a shift, I was doing what all nurses in charge do, I was sitting in the charge nurse's chair at the desk in the ward office pretending to be important and reading the day shift's report, when Nurse Bostock stomped in. She planted her feet and squared up to me; an Amazonian-like woman; when she folded her arms across her chest she almost filled the doorway.

'I'm Nurse Bostock,' she said in a voice like gravel, 'and I'm from Etwall.'

I swallowed hard. Being in charge wasn't supposed to be like this. They never told me what to do about this back at the School of Nursing. I had to work with this creature, all night long, and all on my own. And I was supposed to be in charge. I had to tell her what to do. There was nothing for it, I'd just have to try to be ingratiating. I gave her my most winning smile and said, 'Yeah, I thought it was a real shame about them closing Etwall Hospital.'

Nurse Bostock's pie crust face cracked into a smile and her features seemed to soften. 'Yes,' she said, and uncrossed her arms. She delved into the shopping bag at her feet and produced a giant-sized box of teabags. 'Shall I make us a cup of tea?'

Nurse Bostock and I got on famously for the rest of the shift.

After Etwall I joined the Great Northern Greenway, another cycle route, which had been a railway line once upon a time until Dr Beeching breezed through this corner of Derbyshire brandishing his axe in 1968. I left the cycle track at Mickleover instead of following it all the way into Derby itself. I wanted to make my own way into town because it was thereabouts that I had misspent my youth. Derby could boast not one but two mental hospitals and it was at Pastures Hospital at Micklover and Kingsway Hospital on the ring road where I trained to be a psychiatric nurse in the late 1970s and early 1980s.

Most people become a nurse for the most commendable of reasons: a profound desire to care for others, a wish to give something back to society, a deep need to look after the sick, the disabled, or those who, through no fault of their own, are less fortunate than others. I became a nurse because I *really* fancied the girl in the nursing advert I spotted one day in *The Observer* Sunday colour supplement.

To me she was a vision of state registered loveliness, with her soft, compassionate eyes and her long, dark hair framing her exquisitely sculpted face. Under the caption 'Forget the rat race, join the human race' she was sitting in some sort of a therapy group, leaning forward explaining something, clearly some profound psychiatric insight, to a group of patients who were clustered around her, hanging on to her every word. On the strength of this advert alone I packed in my job as general dogsbody at Eskdale Youth Hostel and dashed off my application form. When I told my girlfriend, who worked in the pub down the road, that

I was going to be a mental nurse she told me she'd always thought a psychiatric hospital would be the best place for me and that she wanted her Abba records back because there was no way she was going to be known as that girl who was going out with the nutter nurse.

After such an inauspicious start and going into nursing for all the wrong reasons I loved my time at Kingsway and Pastures Hospitals (I did my ward experience at Kingsway and my classroom work at Pastures). I must have done quite well too because I even won a prize at the end of my training; I was awarded the accolade of being the second best third year student. I never did get to meet the raven-haired psychiatric nurse of my dreams. Instead I went out with a red-headed Irish nurse called Bernadette who had a temper to match her hair and, all things considered and with the benefit of hindsight of course, I might have faired a whole lot better dating Nurse Bostock.

Gone to the Dogs

The afternoon had become warm and muggy so I stopped for a quick drink at the Nag's Head in Mickleover village. It is a big, old-fashioned pub beside the main road. Back in the days when it had been one of our watering holes, it was the sort of pub where sporty Jag drivers in sheepskin coats and tweed caps would stop off to take their dolly bird girlfriends for gin and tonics. I was once severely ticked off by the senior tutor, after one particularly lively lunchtime session there, for giving one of the girls in our student group a piggyback down the road.

'Don't forget, Student Nurse Richards,' she said to me, peering over her half-moon glasses, 'that the townspeople hereabouts know who you are and what you do. Think very carefully about how your behaviour reflects upon the

Day One, Land's End

Zenner Quoit

*Fish shop –
St Agnes*

Bucks Valley Woods

King Bladud's pigs, Bath

Birmingham Canals

Dovedale

Kinder Scout, a thug of a hill

*Happy Hay
Bales, Crowden*

*Crossing the
M62*

Inside Yearning Saddle Mountain Refuge, the Cheviots

The Falkirk Tunnel

The Falkirk Wheel

Blackrock Cottage & Buachaille Etive Mor, Glen Coe

Crossing the snowfield, Ben Nevis

The Well of Seven Heads

Loch Ness, a grainy indistinct photo

The Wolf Stone at Lothbeg

A9 – The Road to Hell

Journey's end, John O'Groats

profession before you make a spectacle of yourself again.'

Being sure not to make a spectacle of myself, I settled for just an orange juice to slake my thirst then walked towards the town centre, passing Derby City Hospital and where the old Manor Hospital used to be. The Manor had once been a workhouse, a forbidding edifice of soot-stained brick which had been converted into a care of the elderly hospital. I used to take a shortcut through its grounds from Kingsway Hospital to the bus stop. But the Manor had been demolished and was long gone, another victim of health service cuts and over-enthusiastic developers. It had been replaced by a cut-price supermarket, a steakhouse and an Indian takeaway. The demise of the old Manor Hospital in a way summed up so much of what I'd seen on my walk through the Midlands: unloved suburbs, litter strewn streets, dingy takeaways and boarded-up pubs.

When I reached the traffic lights on the ring road I took a left past the fire station and found myself outside the gates of Kingsway Hospital. I had spent five years of my life at Kingsway when I was in my early twenties, five very happy years. Three of them as a student nurse doing my psychiatric nurse training, then two more as a staff nurse working in the day hospital. After what had happened to the Manor I felt a sudden reluctance to look inside the hospital gates and see how time had treated the old place. I've always been told never to go back, that I would be disappointed if I did, things would never be the same, reality fails to live up to that sepia tinted image which exists in your mind's eye. But for some reason, when I did pluck up the courage to walk up the hospital drive, I found that this hadn't seemed to apply to Kingsway. Everything looked exactly as I remembered it. The same broad drive, the same wide lawns, the same mature trees just coming into leaf, and the same squat red brick buildings which were the wards and the main administration block. Beyond the football pitch there were the admission wards, Kingsway House West, which used to be for women, and Kingsway House East, which was for men. And further around to the right and a little closer to the gate was the hallowed ground which was the Female Nurses' Home. I think it best we draw a modest veil over Kingway's Female Nurses' Home and, just for the record, I would like to take this opportunity to categorically refute any of the wicked rumours which may have been circulated that the fragrant, copper-haired Nurse Bernadette ever smuggled me in through a downstairs window after hours.

I suppose it was inevitable that the walk through Derby would turn out to be a stroll through my past and, well, maybe that was the whole point of working my way through the Midlands and ending up in Derby. I've certainly never heard of it being on anyone else's End to End itinerary before. But this End to End was never just about the walk.

So I decided I would stick with the nostalgia theme and head into town via my old route home from work and that would more or less be the end of the Midlands leg of the walk. I worked my way down Albany Road, past the Rowditch pub and along Uttoxeter Old Road. At the junction with South Street I turned right past what used to be Derby Gaol. If the years had treated the Manor Hospital badly and more or less left Kingsway Hospital alone, Derby Gaol, it seemed, had faired the best of the lot.

Derby Gaol was built so solidly that it could have withstood a siege. French revolutionaries may have stormed the Bastille in 1789 but they wouldn't have stood a chance in Derby. On three sides it had tall brick walls covered with green moss that oozed water when it rained. The fourth side was a frontage built of stone which must have been at least three feet thick, with solid stone pillars supporting a gatehouse and set either side of a great oak gate. At each corner sat circular watch towers like massive buttresses. The fortress-like appearance was further enhanced by narrow slits in the walls, the sort which were all the rage in the trendiest of castles during the medieval period. If, in the unlikely event, the gaol should be attacked by a besieging mob advancing along Vernon Street, the prison authorities would have been well equipped to repel all borders.

When I lived just around the corner the gaol hadn't seen service as a prison since 1933, instead it was used as a greyhound track. It was in a pretty rundown state in those days, with damp patches on the walls, mildew and chunks of the rendering flaking off. One of the two watchtowers, I think it was the left-hand one, had tufts of grass and a small tree sprouting from out of the top, but on the other tower, the right-hand one near South Street, the grass would never grow. My landlord took a macabre delight one day in telling me how the grass would never grow on that tower because it was in that grim turret where they would string up the murderers, and that the scaffold and the noose were hanging there still.

As I walked past the remains of the old Derby Gaol on my way into the city centre it was clear that it had undergone quite a facelift. Most of the rotting walls had been demolished, but the formidable frontage, with its columns and turrets, had been saved and made an impressive, if not a little intimidating, gateway to a complex of smart modern offices beyond. On each corner the grim watchtowers remained, their arrow slits looking out like sightless eyes over Vernon Street. It was a whole lot tidier and smarter than I remembered it. The mould and the flaking render had gone and so had all the vegetation. On neither of the two towers was there a stunted tree or a single blade of grass left growing to give any clue as to the fate of those poor souls who had swung and kicked their last in the turrets of Derby Gaol.

The Compleat Angler

Derby marked the end of yet another stage of the walk and after a short break I picked up my route again from where I'd left off.

By this time, in the second year of my End to End, it had more or less replaced for me all that work had previously provided. I was busy, I had long and short-term goals to aim for and I was a heck of a lot fitter. This second year of my trek saw me cover five legs of the walk, from Bath in the south to Kelso just north of the border with Scotland. From early spring until late summer I had either just returned from one leg, was out there walking or was just about to set off on the next leg.

From Derby I set out along Ashbourne Road, past Markeaton Park, went a short way along the Bonnie Prince Charlie Walk (so named because Derby was as far south as the Young Chevalier came before turning around and heading back to Scotland), through Osmaston and on to Ashbourne. Next morning I went via yet another disused railway track to Thorpe and then on to Dovedale.

Before I could set off along Dovedale I had to cross the river via a set of stepping stones. They were a good set of stepping stones, flat and even, and they stuck out well above the water. But it was a long crossing and when I reached the middle it did feel just a little bit exposed. Ahead of me there was a group of three middle-aged walkers, two men and a woman, along with their two dogs. The walkers made their way cautiously across, using their trekking poles to steady themselves over a tricky spot two thirds of the way out, but on the whole they managed very well. The first of their dogs, a rough haired terrier, skipped across as if it were part of a great adventure. But the second dog, a brindle Staffordshire bull terrier, was having none of it. Dog number one ran back across the stepping stones to the middle to see what had happened to his mate then he turned and ran back again, wagging his tail all the way. Dog number two made it out as far as the second stone from the bank, stopped to sniff the water and then jumped back to the bank, where he stood barking at his owners on the far side.

'Come on, Rocco!' the owners shouted from the far bank. But Rocco stayed put. He ran up the bank for fifty yards, couldn't see a way across, then he ran back the other way for fifty yards, still finding no way across.

'Come on, Rocco, it's only a drop of water.' Rocco managed to get his front paws on the first stepping stone but his back legs refused to leave the bank.

'Come on, you big wimp.' Rocco stood and barked at them from the near bank.

'Come on, you won't even get your feet wet.' Rocco threw back his head and let out a pitiful howl.

'Come on, get a move on, you great big wuss.' Rocco assumed a hurt expression and howled even louder.

There was nothing for it. The poor guy had to take his rucksack off, hand his stick to his wife and go back across the stepping stones to retrieve his dog. When he got there he picked Rocco up – he was really too big a dog to be carried – and with a mightily pleased-looking dog in his arms, he cautiously picked his way back across to the far bank again.

The River Dove winds its way through the dale, twisting past limestone crags and pinnacles, between lush green banks and below overhanging trees. It is arguably the loveliest of the Derbyshire dales and, for me, it has always held something of the magic of childhood summers and holidays. I grew up in Sheffield and, with my sister, we were taken out walking by our parents from an early age. There cannot be many greater gifts that a parent can pass on to their children than to start them out rambling. We couldn't afford a car but we could get to places like Castleton or Monsal Dale on the bus. Dovedale, however, was another matter entirely. It was always just a bit too far out, a destination to be dreamed about and lusted after, a place of wonder which could only be visited on high days and holidays. And that is the magic of Dovedale, the queen of all dales; it's a special place, but it's not a dale for working days.

Any visit to Dovedale should be savoured like fine wine and as the afternoon was warm and bright I sat down under a birch tree to drink in just being there. Upstream a heron was stalking, hidden behind some tall reeds. I sat very still to see if it would come closer. A grey wagtail, which was more bright yellow than grey, flitted about the margins of the stream catching flies and taking them to feed its two fledglings. The heron slowly made its way downstream and shooed the wagtails away, so I settled instead for watching the trout rising to take the big yellow mayflies which were landing on the surface of the water.

I'd choose a mayfly when it landed at the top of a smooth glide of water upstream and watch it while it drifted down, taking bets with myself as to how long it would be before the nose of a trout would break the surface of the water and, sometimes with scarcely a ripple, suck it down, then vanish below the gin-clear water again.

It was a day to idle. A day to set aside all worries of miles covered and miles still to go. A time for contemplation. And could there be any better place for that most leisurely of activities than Dovedale, the home of the contemplative man's recreation? If anywhere in England can claim to be the home of angling it is Dovedale. Izaak Walton fished the River Dove in the 1600s with his friend Charles Cotton and together they wrote *The Compleat Angler*, the most famous book ever to be written about fishing. Famous and iconic it may be, but *The Compleat Angler* is not an easy book to read. It takes the form of a conversation between Piscator, an expert fisherman, and Venator (or, later in the book, Viator) a novice angler who is being instructed in the art of fishing. Other characters have walk-on parts such as Aucepts, an otter catcher, and Maudlin the milkmaid. Along with advice about fishing, tackle and baits there are recipes for cooking the fish and brief intermissions while someone interrupts the story to sing a song. But I do have one grumble with old Izaak: he got me into a lot of trouble when I was a lad at school. I liked to go fishing but I didn't like school. I wasn't much of a scholar – come to think of it, I wasn't much of a fisherman either – but it wasn't the usual, wagging off school to go fishing, that I got into trouble for, it was my spelling. After reading *The Compleat Angler*, for years after I was still spelling the word 'complete' the way Walton spelt it. And he earned me more than one set of lines and a couple of periods of detention.

A walk down Dovedale is like a stroll through the pages of *The Compleat Angler*. When I reached Milldale I called at the little 'hole-in-the-wall' shop, bought a cup of tea and a Bakewell slice and sat in the shelter to drink my tea, looking out over the narrow packhorse bridge which spans the river there. But this is not just any old packhorse bridge, this is Viator's Bridge. Poor old Viator, who was already feeling a bit rattled after a tricky descent down the hillside, found the bridge scarily narrow: 'why a mouse can hardly go over it,' quotes Walton in *The Compleat Angler*. 'Tis not two fingers broad.' He draws a veil over how Viator faired with Rocco's stepping stones.

When I was twelve, on one of our rare holiday trips to Dovedale, I was given a severe ticking off by Fat Bertha, who was the first and only female water bailiff I've ever encountered. I don't even know if she was called Bertha, let alone Fat Bertha, that was just the name I made up for her at the time. Bertha was an imposing woman, a small mountain in brown tweed and gum boots. She was so big that you couldn't tell where her bosoms stopped and her belly started. On the left side of her neck she had a vivid purple scar about an inch and half long with a small curly white hair protruding from it. When she was angry this hair vibrated. I can remember that when she was ticking me off all I could do was watch this curly white hair vibrating in a sort of fascinated horror. And what was the crime I had committed which warranted such a stern admonishment? Had she caught me with a creel full of poached river trout or dangling a worm on a hook into Izaak Walton's hallowed waters? No, she saw me playing a game of ducks and drakes, skimming a stone across the surface of the water. I was backed up against a tree and had a grimy sausage-shaped finger wagged in front of my nose. Didn't I realise? she thundered. How could I be so irresponsible? Couldn't I see the harm I might have done? Didn't I realise the pebble I'd just skimmed across the river might have hit a trout on the head and killed it stone dead?

I followed the path across the fields heading for Hartington. Before the path dips down into the village I stopped and looked back. Hidden in the trees on the far side of the river, with only its steeply-pitched roof showing above the branches, is Charles Cotton's Fishing Temple. A little place he had built so he could shelter from the rain and take a break from fishing. I have never been any closer than this view across the river, but they say that the interwoven initials of Charles Cotton and Izaak Walton are carved above the door.

Hartington marked the 500 mile point of the walk so far.

Two Puddings, a Sausage Roll and a Square of Flapjack
'There's no such thing as bad weather' – or so the landlady of the B&B in Hartington said. I was pulling my waterproofs on at the time. 'Only the wrong gear. Well that was what two ramblers who stayed here last week told me,' she said. There's maybe a grain of truth in this but, over the years, I've had too many wettings to go along wholeheartedly with that smug homily. Not that the weather was too bad. There was a fine mist drifting with the breeze which dampened the grass and made the hedgerows look as if Lady Bountiful had been scattering them with her choicest jewels. I set off with my cagoule on but the rain petered out before I'd reached the top of the lane so I stopped and took it off. No sooner had I put the cag away and settled the rucksack back on my shoulders, than the rain started up again and I needed to stop and get the cag back out. And that was the pattern for the morning. I must have put my cagoule on and taken it off a dozen times before I'd worked my way through Middleton-by-Youlgrave, down Bradford Dale, along Lathkill Dale and up the hill to Over Haddon.

I'd planned to stop for a cup of tea at the craft centre in Over Haddon but since my last visit it had closed down and been converted into posh residential apartments. I hadn't had much luck with cups of tea recently so I had to save my thirst until I dropped down the hill and into Bakewell.

The town of Bakewell is famous for having not one but two confectionaries named after it. First of all there is the ever-popular Bakewell tart, so famous that even Mr Kipling had made a version of it. The Bakewell tart has a pastry base, a layer of jam and is topped with almond flavoured sponge. Then there is the Bakewell pudding, rather more of a specialist taste and a pudding with an altogether more dubious and controversial history.

The story, which over the years has taken on all the trappings and mystique of a minor legend, is said to have occurred at the White Horse Inn (which is now the Rutland Arms). The cook made a strawberry tart for dinner which turned out to be a bit of a flop. It sank instead of rising. If she had been a contestant in any of the current TV cooking shows she would have been first to be voted out but as this was some 200 years before the advent of *Master Chef*, she evidently decided she could bluff it out. She served up her pudding and told the poor unsuspecting customers that it was supposed to be like that. And they ate it. Opinions vary as to how much they enjoyed it. When I used to go to Bakewell in my school holidays there was only one shop which claimed to be the purveyors of the 'original' Bakewell pudding; in recent years there have been a whole lot more. It all got a bit silly at one point with threats of lawsuits over who could claim to sell the 'original' Bakewell pudding. There was even talk of taking out a patent on the recipe. That would be one for the history books, the world's first patented pudding. Not wanting to be sued by anyone, I played it safe and bought a sausage roll instead, which I ate leaning over the parapet of the old stone bridge and watching the fat trout swimming in the River Wye.

I left Bakewell via Eweclose, crossing the Monsal Trail and then continuing over the broad meadows towards Hassop. An uneventful but nonetheless pivotal part of the walk because somewhere, while crossing those green pastures with only a sheep or two for company, I passed the same latitude of my home, so all the rest of the walk would be north from where I lived.

From Hassop I climbed Bank Wood, then Bramley Wood and then made the steep descent into Calver. For once I managed to find a café which hadn't been turned into upmarket flats so I ordered a cup of tea quickly before the property developers moved in. Then I followed the River Derwent to Froggatt, Grindleford Bridge and on to Hathersage.

I hadn't fared very well booking somewhere to stay in Hathersage. After my traumas trying to book the Cotswold Way when the National Hunt Festival was on I decided to book the Derbyshire leg of the walk in plenty of time. When I phoned one of the B&Bs in Hathersage the landlady said, 'I'm not taking a booking for *just* one night this early.' Booking B&Bs was proving to be a recurring problem, a lot of them, like Hathersage, made it clear that they didn't want bookings for just one night. A good business strategy for the B&Bs maybe, but bad news for anyone planning a walking tour.

I found somewhere else to stay eventually, but they failed to send me the promised confirmation email and they put me in a poky room with dead bluebottles on the windowsill and empty sachets of shampoo, presumably left by the previous occupant, still littering the shower. In the bar downstairs there was a sign which read, 'As we are on a water meter tap water is chargable'. Next morning the shower, after I'd cleared away the redundant sachets of shampoo, let out a single burst of scalding water and then would produce nothing more than a tepid dribble. So my morning ablutions were reduced to something between a strip wash and a rub down with an oily rag.

At least it got me out and on the road early. It was a bright and sunny morning, perfect walking weather. I crossed the Derwent at Leadmill Bridge and walked the path alongside the river. On the far bank two horses, a piebald and a chestnut, seemed just as thrilled with the morning as I was, they were kicking up their heels and chasing each other around the field.

I left the river at Shatton and went via Wheat Hay Farm to Brough, past the old Roman site of Navio and on to the village of Hope, where there was a sign nailed to a gatepost, written in coloured felt tip pens, asking everyone to look out for a missing grey African parrot, a friendly, talkative chap who answered to the name of Barty Boss.

I didn't see any parrots in Hope, grey or otherwise, but I did become quite chummy with a large white chicken. She had hopped over the wall from the farm next door and into the backyard of the café where I was having an alfresco cup of afternoon tea and square of flapjack. She was a pretty smart and knowing chicken, working her way around under all the tables picking up the crumbs. She gave me one of those quizzical looks which only chickens can produce, cocking her head to one side and quickly sussing out that not only was I chicken-friendly, but also that I was a messy eater, at least when it came to flapjacks. So she came over pretty smartly to clean up under my table. When the café owner came out and shooed her back over the wall and into the farmyard I felt quite lonely so drank my tea up in a bit of a huff and set off walking again.

The afternoon's walk was a steady climb up Wooler Knoll and on to a ridge which runs alongside a plantation of pine trees and then on as far as Hope Cross. Ahead of me, and stopping me in my tracks, was Kinder Scout. It is a bit of a cliché to call a hill dark and brooding, but it's difficult to think of any other way to describe it. Kinder is a grim plateau of gritstone, peat and heather. The 'Dark Peak' in the most literal sense of the words and the home to plane wrecks, mires and foul-smelling bogs. It's a thug of a hill which managed to maintain a threatening presence even on a sunny afternoon when I had been in a holiday humour at coming to the end of the Peak District section of the walk. But there would be no escaping it. Ahead lay the Pennine Way and the first day of the Pennine Way means Kinder Scout. And if Kinder doesn't get you, then Bleaklow surely will.

The Pennine Way: Day One

Sooner or later it happens to every single one of us; every man anyway. It happened to me. Looking back I shouldn't have been taken quite so by surprise, but I was. And it happened to me just a few days before I set out on the Pennine Way. Suddenly, and with not the least inkling of a warning, I turned into my dad.

It all happened on a bright, breezy day. It was too windy for the floppy sun hat I'd been wearing since Land's End to stay on my head. It had blown off twice and twice I'd had to chase after it. The third time it took flight the wind deposited it in a fresh cowpat. It came out dripping and I wasn't going to put it back on my head again, not without a bit of a rudimentary wash anyway, so, hatless, by teatime my head was sunburnt and glowing gently like a Belisha Beacon. What I needed was something a bit more efficient in the headwear department. A hat which would be smart, easy to wear, would keep the sun off the bald bit, the rain off my glasses and would stay put in any sort of a breeze up to, say, Storm Force Ten. At that very moment, suddenly and quite unbidden, a vision of my old dad floated before my very eyes; pipe in his mouth, walking boots on his feet, rucksack on his back and on his head, *a flat cap*. That was it. That's what I needed, that would solve all of my problems; a flat cap. Thanks, dad.

I lost no time making a quick detour to the menswear department of the local Co-op and invested in a sporty little tweed checked number. Cocked at just a bit of an angle and shading my eyes, it looked pretty racy even if I did say so myself. The metamorphosis was complete.

The Pennine Way starts at a pub, The Old Nags Head in Edale, and ends at another pub, The Border Hotel at Kirk Yetholm. It was the first of the UK's long distance National Trails and even though lots of other long trails have been established since the Pennine Way opened in 1965, it remains the walk by which the layman judges the walker.

For all its reputation as the daddy of the long distance footpath, and even though the first day of the Pennine Way has a reputation for walkers dropping out when they realise just what they've let themselves in for, the walk starts with a deceivingly gentle stroll through the Vale of Edale until it reaches Jacob's Ladder, when things start to become a bit more serious.

At one time Jacob's Ladder was considered to be the bad weather option, the main route going up Grindsbrook and crossing the middle of Kinder Scout. My map showed the whole climb onto Kinder as Jacob's Ladder but I had always known it as the short, steep climb above the packhorse bridge beyond Upper Booth. There is a long zigzag out to the left and the story goes that Jacob, who was a pack horse driver, would send his ponies off on this longer zigzag while he took the shorter and steeper path straight up the bank and when he got to the top he'd have time to sit down on a rock and smoke a pipe before his ponies arrived. I followed Jacob's footsteps up the steeper, straighter path and, like Jacob, I had a sit down at the top, only in my case it was to get my breath, not to smoke a pipe.

Jacob's Ladder was only the start, the climb continued unremittingly until the path went over the edge of Kinder, where it levelled out a bit. Kinder Scout has always had a dark reputation, a high moorland plateau roughly frying pan shaped, its edges guarded with crags and rocky outcrops and the centre a glutinous quagmire of soggy brown peat hags. It's a place where the mist can suddenly roll in and what few landmarks there are quickly vanish and the walker becomes disorientated and lost. In fact, throw in a few prehistoric monsters and on a bad day it could be Conan Doyle's *Lost World*. This was why, back when I was a lad, and a mere stripling of a hillwalker, I loved to go up there. I'm not sure I ever really enjoyed floundering through the bogs but I would go up there at any opportunity with my walking mates because, high on adolescent testosterone, we equated hiking over Kinder with toughness and manliness. Maybe we couldn't conquer Everest or climb the north face of the Eiger but at least we could go bog-trotting on Kinder.

In truth the middle of Kinder is best avoided. The Pennine Way follows the edge of the plateau, where the going underfoot is good and the views are much better. Finding a path wasn't a problem, finding the right path was a bit more of a challenge. Paths and trails snaked across the hill in a seemingly random fashion, dotted with an equally random pattern of cairns.

All walkers have had occasion to bless a well-placed cairn, those small piles of stones which make rustic and basic route markers. That sense of relief when a cairn appears out of the mist and confirms that you are not lost after all but are, in fact, on the right track. But you can have too much of a good thing, and there have been places where cairns have proliferated to the extent that, instead of being helpful wayside markers, they have turned walking into a confusing game of join the dots. Newton said that for every action there is an opposite and equal reaction and in the 1970s an underground movement grew amongst some walkers who set out with the express intention of dismantling some of the excessive and confusing cairns, and a few of the well sited useful ones while they were at it. And one day back in the 1970s, on the edge of Kinder, just above Jacob's Ladder, I met two of them.

Beano was the last person I would ever have expected to meet on Kinder Scout. In fact, finding Beano above ground was in itself something of a rarity. Beano was a caver, or potholer, and I worked with him not long after I left school, when I had a job with the Sheffield City Parks Department. He was a compact, barrel-chested man with yellow hair and the pale eyes of an albino, which was how he acquired his nickname. Like most people thus afflicted his eyesight was really poor, so bad I'd seen him hold a book almost up to the end of his nose to read it. But in the dark of a cave his poor eyesight became something of an advantage. He was a caver par excellence and he once took me on a terrifying trip underground, armed with sledgehammers, pickaxes and shovels, to dig out new subterranean tunnels. When we worked together we were supposed to be cutting the grass and looking after the flowerbeds in Sheffield city centre but we spent most of our time riding around on the backs of lorries and nipping into cafés for cups of tea.

Beano was out with his mate Raygold, and they were on a mission to rid Kinder of its surplus cairns. It would be more accurate to say that Raygold was on a mission; Beano was just along for the trip. Whereas Beano was short and stocky, Raygold was tall and rangy with massive hands and arms which hung almost to his knees. He wore a red tee shirt which was a size too small for him, so it was stretched tightly over his chest, and a pair of shorts which were held up with knotted cord around the waist and which had smaller drawstrings knotted tightly around each of his muscular thighs, although what he was worried would go up the leg of his shorts on Kinder Scout, even in summer, seemed unclear.

When he saw a cairn which was deemed to be unnecessary or misplaced Raygold would stoop over it and, with a curiously windmill-like action, his massive hands and long arms would send the stones scattering in every direction while Beano and I had to duck or jump out of the way to avoid the flying rocks.

After a morning's cairn obliteration it was time for lunch. I took out my usual sandwiches and flask but Beano and Raygold had grander ideas. Out of a rucksack they produced a petrol stove, a frying pan, a loaf of sliced bread, a pound of pork sausages and a bottle of Chardonnay. With the minimum of ceremony the cork was pushed into the bottle, the stove was lit and the sausages were fried. We feasted on sausage sandwiches washed down with warm white wine. After lunch and a short siesta they pressed on around the edge of Kinder, destroying cairns as they went, while I cut over towards Grindsbrook, Edale and the train home. I haven't seen Beano and Raygold since that day but judging by the amount of superfluous cairns which have reappeared they must have ceased their activities as self-appointed cairn destructors quite some time ago.

From the path around the edge of the plateau I had superb views towards Kinder Reservoir and, tucked under the hillside itself, a charming little pond known as Mermaid's Pool. The wind was blowing up the edge in a boisterous way and it kept tugging at my cap (which I could still only think of as my dad's cap) and I was worried that it would be blown away before I had even got halfway through the first day. I was grateful then to find some shelter behind the rocks when I reached Kinder Downfall and stopped for lunch.

The Downfall is a tight windy corner where the Kinder River spills over the edge of the plateau and forms a puny waterfall which regularly blows the water back again, with the updraughts soaking the rocks and any unfortunate rambler who happens to be sheltering there. A wet and uncomfortable place it may be, haunted by predatory sheep who are quite prepared to mug you for your sandwiches, yet it has a special place in my affections. I still associate Kinder Downfall with young love because it was on that wind-blasted spot many, many years ago that I had my first ever grown-up snog.

I'd met Liz a couple of weeks earlier at one of the walking club meets. She was a petite, sparky sort of a girl with long auburn hair, a cute face and a pert smile. Goodness knows what she saw in me, a gawky, callow youth whose idea of showing a girl a good time wasn't to take her to the hottest disco in town but out into the wind and rain for a ramble on Kinder. I don't remember much about the walk apart from it being wet, which was usual, and that I got us lost a couple of times. That was also quite usual. At least I managed to find Kinder Downfall and there we found a cosy spot out of the wind and snuggled up together to keep warm. The romance didn't last long. At the end of the summer she went off to teacher training college in some northern town like Huddersfield or Bingley and I went back to the Parks Department and the tender mercies of Beano, Raygold and their mates.

After leaving the romantic idyll of Kinder Downfall the path dropped steeply down to Mill Hill and it was there that I met up with Bryn. Strictly speaking I first saw Bryn just outside Edale, then again a bit later by the packhorse bridge at the foot of Jacob's Ladder. When two walkers are following the same route they constantly overtake then re-overtake each other. One has a break and the other overtakes, then the other has a rest and the first one overtakes. Bryn and I had been passing each other all morning and he wasn't difficult to spot because of his rucksack. Even by Pennine Way standards, where big rucksacks are a common sight, Bryn's backpack was of humongous proportions. He had packed it to bursting point but even then it wasn't big enough; he had a smaller bag strapped to the outside, a big, square-shaped camera bag slung around his shoulders and still he didn't have room for his water bottle. He had to carry that in his hand.

As I dropped down off Kinder I saw Bryn ahead of me, standing under a signpost studying his map. He folded his map away and set off towards Hayfield in a purposeful manner. By the time I reached the signpost he was back there again, studying his map. We compared notes and set off together across the slabs from Mill Hill to the Snake Road. He told me he was from Surrey and that he'd walked the West Highland Way last year so he was having a crack at the Pennine Way this time and he planned to camp all the way.

By the time we reached the A57 Snake Road we were

both ready for a breather but it was already 3.15pm and I was becoming worried about the time. The first day of the Pennine Way crosses two big hills: Kinder, which was behind us by this point, and Bleaklow, which was still ahead. And while Bryn could just pitch his tent if night fell I knew I'd have to get across Bleaklow to Crowden and even then I'd still a couple of miles of roadwalking before I reached my B&B. We agreed to press on, each at our own pace.

I set off up Devil's Dyke, passing the Wainstones to the left. It took me an hour to reach Bleaklow Head, where I decided I'd earned an afternoon break. Ten minutes later Bryn passed me, going strongly. Forty-five minutes after that, by John Track Well, I caught up with Bryn when he stopped for a break. He looked as if he was settling in. He'd spread his gear out on the heather, unpacked his Swiss Army knife, a plate, a mug, a big hunk of cheese and a packet of cream crackers. I wondered if he was going to stay there for the night and put his tent up. I'd still got a way to go and I showed him on my map where the B&B I was heading for was.

'But that's miles away,' said Bryn. He seemed genuinely horrified.

'Well it's not too bad,' I said. 'Just down the road a bit, past the Devil's Elbow.'

'It's at least three miles beyond Crowden.'

'I couldn't get in anywhere nearer. The youth hostel and the other B&Bs were full.'

'That's the beauty of having a tent,' he said and patted his bulging rucksack.

'I'd better get going then,' I said.

'Absolutely, you don't want to be benighted up here.'

I left him, feeling a bit chastened, and picked my way through the heather on the narrow airy path along the edge of Torside Clough, with the lights of Crowden winking in the distance. Perhaps he was right. Old hands at the Pennine Way love to tell stories of the first day out, epic tales of walkers wandering aimlessly for miles lost in the boggy wastes of Kinder and Bleaklow. It was a tough enough walk to Crowden, wasn't I being a bit daft adding an extra couple of miles on that? My legs were beginning to stiffen and the soles of my feet were feeling as if someone had spent a couple of hours beating them with a stick. It always came back to the old debate: tent versus B&B, light pack versus heavy pack. What it boiled down to was just how far would you be prepared to go for a comfy bed, a hot meal and a pint or two of beer at the end of the day. I hitched my pack up on my shoulders. In my case, quite a long way.

The Pennine Bitter Men

Next morning I had to trek back up the road for a couple of miles before I reached the Pennine Way again. But it was a bright morning and the walk up the road around the Devil's Elbow seemed like a gentle warm-up for the main event. There also seemed to be something of a change in me, a spring in my step, and even my pack seemed lighter. I was starting to notice the things around me, like the foxgloves by the roadsides and the birds singing in the trees. I was feeling freer, more relaxed. I hadn't felt like this the day before, I'd felt weighed down and leaden-legged. Maybe all those horror stories about the first day of the Pennine Way had been lodged somewhere deep in my unconscious. I think I had been more tense and worried about the previous day's walk than I realised. But now that dreaded first day was behind me.

In my newly-liberated state I stopped and looked over

the wall and took in the view across the valley; the patchwork of green fields and slate-blue reservoirs. I counted all the reservoirs I could see from that spot alone. There were five. The southern part of the Pennines is studded with them. I had a look at the map and counted up the blue, angular-shaped patches. Today's route would take me past at least eleven of them.

I was back on the Pennine Way itself by ten o'clock and walking over the dam wall of Torside Reservoir then through a turnstile and across the A628 Woodhead Pass Road. Then it was a long climb through the heather, up the valley towards Laddow Rocks. The heather was in bloom and at its best and I kept stopping to look at the view back the way I'd come, towards Torside Clough, where the hills had a smoky purple hue about them. Every few minutes a low-flying passenger jet would cruise overhead, stacked in a queue waiting to land at Manchester Airport.

I found myself wondering how Bryn was getting on. Had he camped out on the hill after I left him or had he pressed on to Crowden? I assumed he was somewhere ahead of me. Campers tend to make early starts whereas I'd had a late breakfast and an extra cup of coffee and then I had the additional miles to make up along the road before I was back at Crowden.

When I reached Laddow Rocks I started to be dive-bombed by clouds of slow-moving black flies. They were everywhere. About three quarters of an inch long, half asleep and very dopey. They seemed to find their way into everything – ears, nose, mouth – I even found two squashed in my sock when I took my boot off that evening. They seemed intent on either flying down ramblers' throats or, failing that, mating with each other. They would couple at the rear and then go backwards and forwards in a push-me, pull-you fashion. Goodness knows what they found to eat up there.

The path became broken, more indistinct and boggy around where it joined the upper reaches of Crowden Great Brook. I overtook a couple who, I discovered later, were from Belgium. They were picking their way over the wet ground then, with a cry of delight, they came across a path of stone slabs leading up to Black Hill.

Few hills have less charm than Black Hill, a featureless mound of dark peat and bog. Its summit is a small heap of rocks with a trigpoint on top known as Soldier's Lump. And it's fortunate that this pile of stones is the highest point because if they had tried to put a trigpoint anywhere else on that soggy hill it would have keeled over and sunk without trace. It had been more years than I cared to remember since I had last been on Black Hill and stone slabs had been laid to make the path since then, which had improved matters no end. The slabs made it a walk, instead of a flounder through the peat, but I still can't think of any compelling reason which would make me want to rush back up there again.

As I trudged up Black Hill I amused myself trying to remember the names of the four 'Pennine Bitter Men'. It would be in the mid-1970s when four guys who I knew from the Good Companions Rambling Club in Sheffield set out to walk the Pennine Way. I was in my late teens at the time and working at Eskdale Youth Hostel in the Lake District. My mother would write to me each week and send me a bulletin on their progress. It was she who had named them 'The Pennine Bitter Men', (they all enjoyed a drink and Webster's Pennine Bitter was a popular beer back in those days). Jack Presley was their leader, and it was he who had first introduced me to the grim delights of bog-trotting over Kinder Scout. He decided to get his Pennine Way expedition together to help fill the time while his wife Dorothy flew over to Australia to visit their son, who had emigrated out there, and to meet the grandchildren she had never seen. Ernest Hatcliffe was second in command; a tall, white-haired and distinguished-looking man, he was the oldest and would have been well over seventy at the time. When he wasn't hillwalking Ernest had made quite a name for himself locally as a ballroom dancer. Then there was the quietly-spoken George Wild. I was good mates with his son Ronnie. I was racking my brains to remember the fourth member then it came to me just as I reached the summit of Black Hill. He was Harry Dyson, a Geordie who, as I remember, was an avid Roy Orbison fan. They walked the Pennine Way in three weeks, mostly staying in youth hostels, and at the end of it were able to boast that they hadn't suffered one single blister between them.

Teenagers tend to be singularly unimpressed by the exploits of their father's generation but I was (and still am) impressed by The Pennine Bitter Men. I think I even got around to sending Jack Presley a postcard from the Lakes to congratulate them (at least I hope I did). They had set an example and they made me want to emulate them. After The Pennine Bitter Men, the Pennine Way was always going to be an intrinsic part of my End to End.

The walk down from Wessenden Head was a delight and the day had turned out bright, but not too hot – perfect walking weather in fact. Then it was on past Black Moss Reservoir. I leaned on the bridge overlooking this calm sheet of blue water listening to a skylark. Hard to imagine the havoc and carnage this peaceful patch of water caused when the dam burst one stormy night in 1810, flooding the valley below and drowning six people.

I crossed the A62 and then followed a small section of the Pennine Bridleway to my B&B at Bleak Hey Nook (or Bleaky-Nook as the locals call it). It was like a gathering of Pennine Way walkers. There was Anna and Dirk, the

Belgian couple I'd met on the hill just above Laddow Rocks. Dirk was tall and dark-haired, Anna small and outspoken. They came over to the UK each year to walk one of the long distance footpaths. Walking in the opposite direction, north to south, were Neil and his son Martin, from Sheffield, and in that uncanny way which often happens on a trek, I discovered they lived just around the corner from where I was brought up in Sheffield. Nobody had seen anything of Bryn.

Stoodley Piked

I'm not the quickest of starters in the morning but somehow I was the first away from the B&B. There was a short stretch of Pennine Bridleway then it was back to the Pennine Way proper and moorland walking over Close Moss and White Hill, where a tiny meadow pipit perched on the dry stone wall and then kept flying along and landing again, keeping pace with me.

The footbridge over the M62 trans-Pennine motorway has become something of a Pennine Way icon. I couldn't resist stopping in the middle and waving to the traffic. A juggernaut hooted back at me.

I walked up onto Blackstone Edge, where there was an industrial air to the scenery in that part of the Pennines. The rock was gritty and blackened sandstone, the route crossed by A roads at regular intervals and the whole area dotted with small angular reservoirs. Power lines looped across the hills and on the edge of the moors grimy-looking industrial villages crowded into narrow valleys. Away to the west I could see an industrial sprawl which must have been Oldham and Rochdale.

Even though it was only late morning there wasn't a lot of bounce left in my stride. My legs felt heavy and leaden.

Maybe because it was the third day of heavy walking and the pace was beginning to catch up with me. I passed the Aiggin Stone, a medieval guidestone for travellers, and turned left along a short stretch of Roman road with a stone gutter running down the centre. When I reached the A58 (the fourth major road crossing of the day) I had intended to just press on and try and walk off my tiredness but my willpower weakened at the sight of the pub, the White House. I'm not sure that stopping for a pint of Theakstons and a packet of cheese and onion crisps helped my tiredness any, but it made me feel a whole lot more cheerful about the prospect of the afternoon's walk.

In the distance I could see Stoodley Pike. It stood high on the ridge above Hebden Bridge looking a bit like a dumpy church steeple, but with no church underneath it. On a clear day, as it was, you could see it from miles away. It has the knack of beckoning you ever onwards yet never seeming to get any closer. I pressed on over Chelburn Moor and past three more reservoirs as the sun came out and the afternoon warmed up. Still Stoodley Pike was there, beacon-like, tantalising, ahead of me. I was beginning to feel under a bit of pressure. I was staying at a farm on a ridge above Hebden Bridge and Martin, one of the walkers staying at Bleak Hey Nook with me the previous night, had told me that the only pub which did meals was a mile away from the farm and that they stopped serving food quite early. But it hadn't seemed very important at the time and I couldn't remember just when it was that he said they stopped serving.

I was more than ready for a breather when I finally did reach Stoodley Pike. I couldn't read the inscription because the bright sun was throwing the words into deep shade. I did know that Stoodley Pike called itself a 'peace monument'. It was finished in 1815 after the Battle of

Waterloo and developed a bad habit of collapsing whenever war was declared, like it did in 1854 when war was declared with Russia, then it was rebuilt in 1856 when peace was restored. I would have liked to linger but knew that I didn't have time so I headed down into the valley and passed a farm which was more like a charnel house. It had a grisly heap of bits of dead sheep piled up in the middle of the yard and it was attracting an impressive swarm of bluebottles.

The valley just above Hebden Bridge, near Callis Wood, is a tight wooded cleft, yet they still managed to squeeze into this narrow gap a railway line, a river, a main road and the Rochdale Canal. I crossed all four of these as quickly as I could and started to climb up the other side of the valley on a steep narrow path of stone slabs which wound its way between the houses. Halfway along there was a tiny disused cemetery with moss-covered gravestones tilted at crazy angles, Gothic statues of angels and walls overgrown with ivy. If it had been a wild and spooky night, instead of a warm summer afternoon, it would have been the perfect atmospheric backdrop for a spot of *Hammer House of Horror* goings-on. As it was I couldn't help looking over my shoulder, half expecting to see Vincent Price with fangs and a long dark cloak drifting out from behind one of the crumbling mausoleums, or Peter Cushing, as Van Helsing, stalking past armed with a mallet and a stake of wood.

But it wasn't the fangs of Dracula that were worrying me at that moment, it was trying to sort out the route on that tangled hillside and getting to the B&B and then out again to the pub before they stopped serving evening meals. And the problem wasn't finding a route, it was which route to choose for not only do they manage to cram every conceivable form of transport into that narrow valley, they've also found space for the Pennine Bridleway, the

Pennine Way: official route and the Pennine Way: Wainwright's alternative. My map had them all marked but it didn't differentiate which was the official route and which was Wainwright's variation on a theme. It was hot, my shirt was sweaty and sticking to my back and I was fretting about missing my meal. I resorted to my usual default position at times like these: my Headless Cross mode. I followed one route up the hill for ten minutes (I'm still not sure which one it was), decided it was going the wrong way, backtracked, followed the other route uphill for ten minutes, decided that was wrong as well, came back again and tried the only option that was left, the Pennine Bridleway. I followed that for ten minutes and still wasn't sure it was right but by this time I was late and running out of options so decided I had better keep going. Just as I had come to the conclusion that I was destined to wander the slopes above Hebden Bridge forever like a landlocked Flying Dutchman I came across a Pennine Way sign pointing out across a field (it didn't specify whether it was Wainwright's or the official route). Like a drowning man lunging for a piece of driftwood I struck out across the field ignoring the Charolais bull, who seemed more interested in the cows anyway, but had less luck with a couple of bullocks (the hoodies of the bovine world) who decide they wanted to see me off. By this point I was cross, hot and sweaty, my face was streaked with mud and my cap awry. I was in no mood to stand for any nonsense from a couple of adolescents so I told them, in short order, how nice they would look sizzling on a barbeque with a dollop of English mustard and a crisp side salad. Then, after I'd waved my trekking pole under their noses, they were quickly galloping back across the field to daddy with chastened expressions on their long furry faces.

I came out onto the road on the top of an exposed and

windy ridge and from there it was a short distance to the farm where I was staying. As I arrived hot, sweaty and panting, the farmer was putting out the wheelie bin by the gate. I wasn't sure whether to expect an effusive welcome; this was Yorkshire after all.

'Hello,' I said. 'I'm Robin, I'm booked in for B&B tonight.'

He took a long slow look at me, taking in the sweat-soaked shirt and mud-spattered appearance. 'Aye,' he said, 'we wondered where you'd got to.'

I dumped my gear in my room and, dragged a comb through my hair, as quickly as I could, and, after apologising to the farmer's wife for my hasty departure, dashed off to try and get something to eat.

There was a walled lane beside the farm which dipped down the far side of the hill. I wasn't at all sure of the way to the pub and, rather foolishly, I'd left my map back at the farm. I might have missed the lane off to the left altogether if it hadn't been for a group of cyclists riding along it. As it was, I followed them and in five minutes I was at Jack's Bridge and the pub, The New Delight. I reached the bar and, trying not to sound too out of breath, asked the landlady if they were still serving food. She looked pointedly at her watch, then at the clock on the wall, then back at me, and then she smiled and handed me a menu from under the bar. 'Just in time,' she said.

Wet and Dry

Next morning I had my first taste of proper Pennine Way weather. It had been overcast and windy when I left the B&B with just a little light rain over Heptonstall Moor. I'd put my waterproof jacket on but had resisted wearing my overtrousers because, and this is the case for every walker

141

I know, they are the most loathed piece of rambling kit. Pulling on overtrousers, especially when you are wearing boots, is the quickest way known to man of smearing mud from ankle to groin, they restrict your movement and they make an irritating swishing noise of nylon on nylon as you walk along.

When I reached Lower Walshaw Reservoir I watched a young Canada goose trying to navigate its way across a slatted aluminium bridge. It couldn't quite work out how it could stand on the bridge yet still see through to the water below. It would take two steps then a jump and flap its wings, a couple more steps then another wing-flapping leap. It made it to the other side and, with a backward glance at the offending structure, stretched its wings and flew off.

The wind was getting stronger and blowing me along from behind at a merry pace. It was quite fun surfing the breeze and took all the effort out of walking. Almost as if a big imaginary hand was under my bum half lifting and half pushing me up the hill. Then the note of the wind changed for a second from a steady roar to sudden dead calm followed, a fraction of a second later, by a whoosh like the opening of a floodgate as a squall, which I swear consisted of a solid mass of water, hit me from behind, soaking me in an instant, from my waist down to my sock tops. Streams of water cascaded from the cuffs of my trousers down my legs and pooled in my boots, which started to make a squelching sound as I walked along. And I began to affect a curious bow-legged cowboy like walk, a bit like a toddler who's wearing a wet nappy. Then the squall switched itself off, like someone turning off a power shower, and, with the brisk wind still blowing from behind, my legs and bum were dry again, if a little chapped and chaffed, before I'd reached Top Withens.

It wasn't difficult to imagine Heathcliff and Cathy acting out their tragic love story up there. Top Withens is a ruined farm, isolated on a windblown hill with just a couple of stunted trees for company. If you're Emily Brontë, and you're looking for an evocative location to set your steamy new novel about love and revenge and all the things you shouldn't really know very much about because you're a vicar's daughter and had led a sheltered life, then you couldn't do much better than Top Withens. And with the wind and squally showers it was looking its lonely, dramatic, windblown best. I'd like to have asked the two Japanese girls who had made the pilgrimage up there what they thought about it but they didn't have much English and I have even less Japanese. The Brontës are really popular in Japan. Even the signposts around Top Withens are in Japanese as well as English.

If I was unlucky with a surprise wetting up by Walshaw Reservoir I was lucky with the rain above Cowling. For once I had a bit of warning that the weather was about to change. I was walking past a small shooting lodge when the wind became suddenly gusty and the sky in the east took on a purple hue like the colour of an angry bruise. The lodge was locked and shuttered but there was a small lean-to attached to it without a door and it promised a safe haven from the storm. It was full of logs, old lumber and fire-beaters but I squeezed inside just as a flash of lightning split the sky and the hillside opposite disappeared behind sheets of rain and sleet.

There is something very cosy about being tucked away somewhere warm and dry when there is wild weather raging outside. I'd expected the storm to quickly blow itself out but it began to settle into its stride and I watched as my route turned from a path to a stream, from a stream to a river and then from a river to a torrent. I soon became bored watching the weather so I did a little bit of furniture removing, shifted a couple of bits of old splintery wood, made myself a tolerably comfortable seat and settled down to sit out the storm. I'd long since given up the idea of carrying a book with me and so I was reduced to reading the edges of my map to pass the time.

There was a surprising amount of useful info all arranged under subheadings and filling up the empty spaces on my map. There was a section giving a brief history of the walk and explaining how it was the brainchild of a man called Tom Stephenson. If there is one man who deserves to be up there in every walker's Hall of Fame it is Tom Criddle Stephenson. He had a long and illustrious career as a freelance journalist and campaigner for countryside issues. He served on national bodies like the Ministry of Town and Country Planning, the National Parks Commission and he was secretary of the Ramblers' Association for years. He first floated the idea for the Pennine Way back in 1935 in a, now famous, article for the *Daily Herald*, 'Wanted: A Long Green Trail'. The idea was just the start. It took thirty years of campaigning, negotiation and sheer hard work before the Pennine Way opened in 1965. He lived to be ninety-four, finally hanging up his rambling boots in 1987.

The rain was still pouring but I was snug (and smug) and dry in my shelter, so I carried on reading the information panels on my map.

The Pennine Way proved a great success but as much of it was over soft peaty hills and moorland, and as it tended to enjoy the sort of weather which I was sheltering from, the 'Long Green Trail' quickly became a muddy brown swamp. In an effort to find something that resembled solid ground, walkers would spread out away from the path itself and as a result the original track of the

Pennine Way became a broad, sludgy and eroded scar across the hillside. I have known walkers who became lost in the mist on the Pennine Way and have gone around in circles only to discover, when the fog cleared, that even though they had been lost and going around in ever-decreasing circles, because the path was so wide, they had never actually left the footpath. The Pennine Way quickly gained a reputation for not being a walk any more, but as an endurance test for anyone who enjoyed being in bog up to their knees for an extended period, and for people who considered trenchfoot to be something of a badge of honour. In the late 1980s and early 1990s an initiative was started to lay tracks of flagstones which had been salvaged from the old mills being demolished across the north of England. The flagstone paths were built on the lines of the old stone causeys like the ancient packhorse routes. The flagstone tracks weathered nicely, the erosion scars on the hills began to heal and walking the Pennine Way became a whole lot nicer and I'd been very glad of these slabs already on the walk. But not everyone was happy. The 'muck-and-bullets' brigade – the old-time Pennine Way walkers – thought that the flagstones made it too easy and they wouldn't miss any opportunity to tell modern Pennine Way walkers what it was like in their day.

At last I could look out of my shelter and see the hillside opposite. The rain had almost stopped so I folded my map away and walked on to Lothersdale, where I found Anna and Dirk, looking a bit damp, sitting on a bench outside the Hare and Hounds pub.

Anna was reading in her Pennine Way guidebook about how the responsible walker should always carry a small shovel with them in case they get caught out in the hills and need to do what bears have become famous for doing in the woods. If they are thus armed with a shovel then they

145

can dig a small hole and bury it. Anna was not impressed.

'Take a shovel?' she said. 'Take a shovel? Have you ever seen a sheep with a shovel?'

The Pen-y-ghent Café

The youth hostel at Malham was full to bursting. At breakfast next morning I sat next to Mike, who was walking the Pennine Way north to south. Over cornflakes he told me, and everyone else sitting at our table for that matter, how he had left Kirk Yetholm just a week ago and planned to be in Edale by the following Wednesday. That would be eleven days for the whole Pennine Way and good going by anybody's standards (I was expecting to take nearer three weeks). Not only that, but he was carrying a full pack and all his camping gear. I'm sure that covering the ground in the quickest possible time was not what Tom Stephenson had in mind when he first thought up the Pennine Way but I did have a bit of sympathy for Mike. He told me how he worked as a school teacher in Suffolk and that just before the start of the long school summer holiday, his girlfriend, also a teacher, had dumped him and he was faced with the prospect of a long, bleak summer vacation stretching out in front of him.

'I didn't know what I was going to do with myself all summer,' he said.

'You didn't think of joining the French Foreign Legion?' said a large, rather imposing-looking woman, with her grey hair scraped severely back in a bun net. She was sitting at the end of the table eating a pot of strawberry yoghurt.

'I thought about that first,' said Mike, casting only the briefest of glances in her direction. 'But then I thought no, I'll

146

do the Pennine Way instead, that'll keep me out of mischief.'

'If you've got all summer holiday,' said the woman, scraping the inside of the pot so she didn't miss the last trace of yoghurt, 'why are you rushing to finish it so quickly?'

'Oh well,' said Mike, 'I was buying a new tent before I set off and there was this cute girl working in the camping shop. We went out a couple of times before I set off so now I'm going as quick as I can so I can get back and be with her.'

Mike finished his breakfast as quickly as he could and set off south dreaming of his siren of the camping shop and I set off north with thoughts of Malham Cove, Fountain's Fell and Pen-y-ghent.

For once I had a deadline. I'd promised to meet Nick, my brother-in-law, on the summit of Pen-y-ghent at three o'clock. Nick first came to Yorkshire on school trips led by Mr M. P. Davis, his charismatic geology and geography teacher. Mr Davis would bring his class up to Horton-in-Ribblesdale for a field trip then he would stay on after his boys went back home to take part in, and usually to win, the Yorkshire Three Peaks Run over Pen-y-ghent, Ingleborough and Whernside.

Malham seemed to be in a black hole as far as mobile phone signals were concerned and although I'd tried texting Nick he had no idea whether I was on schedule, and I had no idea where he was. During breakfast at the youth hostel the warden had read the weather forecast out to us all: fine, light winds with maybe a little high cloud. No mention of rain, so I felt a bit miffed when I got to Tennant Gill and it started to drizzle. I tried texting Nick again from the summit of Fountains Fell, despite the clucking of a group of ramblers, apparently purists. A couple of them even went as far as unplugging their iPods from their ears to make pointed remarks to each other about people disturbing the peace of the countryside with their mobile phones.

At least it was clear and so meeting up with Nick wouldn't be a problem. I looked across the valley to the singular outline of Pen-y-ghent with its scarp and dip slopes. Surely I could get across there and be on the summit before three o'clock?

In the end I was late, but only quarter of an hour late. As I came down into the valley from Fountain's Fell the drizzle increased to light rain. I was already wearing my cagoule so, standing beside the aptly named Rainscar Farm, I put the waterproof cover on my rucksack to try and keep the contents dry. Then, two minutes further down the road, the light rain became heavy rain so I stopped and pulled my overtrousers on. Two minutes after that Pen-y-ghent modestly drew a blanket of mist and rain over herself and the visibility dropped to almost nil. My hopes of meeting Nick on the top plummeted. My glasses became fogged by the rain, faces became blurred and other walkers became fuzzy indistinct outlines in hoods and cagoules. I followed the steep path to the summit, never being able to see more than a few feet of track in front of me.

There was no question of a view from the summit, just the question of whether Nick was there or not. I wandered around the summit cairn trying to wipe the rain off my glasses with a soggy tissue and peering as closely as I could at the faces of the other damp walkers huddled in whatever shelter they could find. As none of them appeared to be my brother-in-law I decided the best policy was to head down to Horton-in-Ribblesdale. He knew I was following the Pennine Way route and there was nothing to be gained by staying on the top and getting wetter and wetter.

I looked closely at each walker who were making their

way up until I dropped below the mist somewhere around Pen-y-ghent Side and when I reached the crossroads near Hunt Pot I found the lean figure of Nick sitting under the signpost waiting with his video camera to film me as I walked down the hill. When the mist dropped he had realised there was no point trying to find me on the summit and knowing I'd have to pass by the crossroads it had seemed the obvious place to wait.

We walked down into Horton together and he treated me to a pint mug of tea in the famous Pen-y-ghent Café, the home of the Yorkshire Three Peaks Walk. There were a few Three Peaks walkers noisily celebrating their success at the far end of the café. We also had cause for celebration: Horton-in-Ribblesdale was, for me, the halfway point between Land's End and John O'Groats.

Boots, Beer, Brass Bands, and Bogs

It felt like Judgement Day and I was the last one up. The breakfast tables in the Crown Hotel at Horton-in-Ribblesdale were littered with half-eaten bowls of cornflakes, toast crumbs, dirty pots and coffee mugs tipped on their side dribbling coffee. All the signs of a rushed and hasty departure. It must have had something to do with all the door slamming, loo flushing and rapid thudding of boots down the stairs which had woken me up at five o'clock in the morning.

My plate of bacon and eggs was slung onto the table in front of me by a sullen youth who plainly resented having to serve up two breakfast sittings. One for the fit types, setting out on the Yorkshire Three Peaks Challenge, and another one for the solitary End to Ender who had no intention of going outdoors until the streets were well and truly aired.

At least the Three Peakers had a good day for their walk. The sun was warm, the birds were singing, Pen-y-ghent, across the valley, had thrown off her mantle of early morning mist and walking was a delight. I took a breather halfway up Long Mires to look across the valley at the Ribblehead Viaduct. The industrial revolution may have given us dark satanic mills but the coming of the railways blessed us with some of the most graceful and monumental railway viaducts, and none more so than Ribblehead with its multiple arches spanning the valley. Then, as I watched, and as if on cue, a steam train chugged across the viaduct, trailing a plume of white smoke like a comet.

The day's walk was mostly along good broad tracks with fantastic views over open ridges like Cam High Road, but when I arrived in Hawes it was clear the town was under siege. The streets were packed with happy, rucksack-toting people all wearing bright blue tee shirts bearing the legend 'Black Sheep Boots and Beer Walking Festival'. Every café, every tearoom and every pub was packed to the doors with people wearing blue boots and beer tee shirts. I saw two faces I recognised in the crowd, the only ones without blue tee shirts on. It was Anna and Dirk.

'See,' said Anna, shouting to me over the throng, 'none of them have shovels.'

I managed to fight my way to the bar in the White Hart and ordered a pint of Black Sheep. If you can't beat 'em, join 'em, I thought. The barmaid, flustered by the crush of customers, gave me my beer, took the money I was proffering and then handed my change to another customer.

The town didn't just seem to be hosting the Boots and Beer Festival, there also seemed to be some sort of a convention for blokes who build those cars that you can put together yourself, like the one Patrick McGoohan used to drive in the opening credits of *The Prisoner*. Next morning, when I saw a labrador wearing a Boots and Beer tee shirt I knew it was time to quit the town.

Where the path went down by the river I saw a walker climbing over the stile near the bridge. There was something familiar about him. It was the way he walked with a slight sideways stagger and the outline of the massive pack on his back.

'Bryn!' I couldn't believe it. 'How are you, Bryn?' I said.

He lifted his eyes from the ground just in front of his feet and just for a moment they focused on mine. 'Suffering,' he said.

'I haven't seen you,' I said, 'not since way back on Torside Clough.'

'Oh I got to Crowden,' he said, 'and I camped there. They made me a meal at the youth hostel but I was so knackered I stopped there for two nights and had a rest day. But since then I've had to do twenty miles every day to make up the time. But I've bought a new stove and some stuff to put on my blisters so I think I'll be all right ...'

His voice tailed off and he resumed walking again with small purposeful steps, his eyes focused on the ground and his shoulders hunched under the weight of his mammoth pack.

I'd promised myself a short detour to see Hardraw Force, said to be Britain's highest waterfall (above ground). Access is, rather uniquely, via the bar of the Green Dragon Inn. The sacrifices we End to Enders are forced to make. It was, to be honest, a touch early, even for me. They were still clearing up after breakfast. At the back of the pub I crossed a couple of fields, past the bandstand, then paid a small fee to get into a rocky cove where a single spout of water spills over the edge to free fall before crashing onto the stones below. All the more impressive because it feels enclosed, hemmed into a natural amphitheatre with the sound of the water thundering and reverberating back from the rocky walls.

After taking some photos I headed back past the bandstand, mindful that I hadn't really started the day's walk. Hardraw is only a mile from Hawes, and I still had Great Shunner Fell to tackle.

Next to the bandstand, behind the Green Dragon at Hardraw, they had erected a beer tent and I found myself in the middle of the Hardraw Scar Brass Band Contest (honestly I was beginning to feel that my walk was being stalked by festivals and events of one sort or another). The field had filled up with spectators, mostly older people who were settling in for the long haul – they had come equipped with deckchairs, blankets and flasks of tea. The first band, sharply turned out in maroon blazers and dark trousers with knife-edge creases, filed onto the bandstand. The soloist, a trumpeter, raised his instrument to his lips, puffed out his cheeks and filled the air with pure brassy tones.

I could cheerfully have stayed there all day, given Great Shunner Fell the elbow and stretched out on the grass in the warm sun, listening to the brass bands with a cool pint of beer in my hand. But instead I had to pick up my rucksack, turn my back on the music and point my feet in the direction of the next big hill, just occasionally catching a snatch of the music when it drifted across on the breeze.

As a walk, Great Shunner Fell was just a slog with nothing to commend it. My mood wasn't improved any when I was overtaken by a young couple wearing tee shirts and plimsolls. I'd first encountered them earlier in the day when I was walking from Hawes to Hardraw. The young man stopped me to ask about the path up Great Shunner Fell. They were not dressed for hillwalking. Every year people underestimate the British hills and get into difficulties by not being properly kitted out and not having decent boots on, so I was a bit evasive about the route and referred them to the Tourist Information Office in Hawes. She was blonde, slim and pretty and he had a cocky air about him. He grinned too much and a bit too widely. When they overtook me, springing from rock to rock like two young gazelles, his grin became even wider. With a pointed look towards me he whispered something to his girlfriend, which I couldn't hear for the wind. She looked at me and burst out laughing. There was no way I could keep up with them so I just had to keep slogging on at my own pace as they moved further and further ahead.

The path was, for the most part, pretty good with stone slabs over the boggy bits. At about the halfway point the slabs ended. I think they must have run out of slabs. It's a shame they didn't have just a couple of extra ones because between where the slabs finished and quite a decent stony path started was a yard or two of black pulsating swamp with a couple of half-submerged stepping stones poking out of the mire. I stepped cautiously onto one of the stones. It wobbled alarmingly. To try and keep my balance I put my other foot on what looked like a patch of firm ground. It wasn't. It was gloopy peat which sucked my foot down almost as far as my knee. With arms and legs flailing around I somehow managed to pull my leg out of the sludge and flounder for a couple of steps until I reached the stony path, where I stopped to survey the damage. My right foot was fine. My left was covered in black primeval slime which was oozing down and beginning to form an obnoxious-smelling pool around my boot. It wasn't so much getting a wet foot which bothered me, it was that I had somehow managed to stumble into a bog on a fine day and even where there were slabs. Well there wasn't a lot I could do about it up there on the hill so I just had to scrape off the excess gunge with a bit of stick and press on. The walk developed a new soundtrack as I headed towards the summit: my right foot went clump, my left foot went squelch.

My mood wasn't helped, shortly after, by seeing the boy and girl sitting grinning at me from the summit shelter, swigging pop out of a bottle and stuffing themselves with crisps. I noticed their white plimsolls were still pristine.

When I was younger I could keep pace with the best of them going up a hill but not any more. I'd noticed this sort of thing had happened quite a lot on the walk. Some young buck streaks past on the way up a hill. He glances back at me with a look of pity as I slowly labour along and then when you reach the top of the hill he is lounging there by the summit cairn tucking into his sandwiches. But by this point of the walk I had developed my own strategy to deal with this rather uneven set of events, a feeble attempt to pull some tattered shreds of dignity around the hunched shoulders of the ageing hillwalker, and I used it as best I could that afternoon. I would approach the summit cairn going at a steady even pace. I would wave and shout 'Hi!' as brightly as I could then, even if my legs were crying out for a break, I'd just press on over the summit, past the cairn and onwards down the hill without even breaking step. Having a rest on the summit is for wimps. It worked very nicely that afternoon. He choked on his crisps.

Dickens and the Bowes Loop

Next morning the cloud was down and soon after I set off walking the light rain turned into a heavy downpour. But somehow this weather seemed quite appropriate because I was off over the moor for a visit to the Tan Hill Inn, Britain's highest pub and the only pub I've ever known with its very own snow tractor parked outside.

The Tan Hill seemed to attract a singular bunch of patrons. Just to get indoors I had to climb over a sheep which had positioned herself across the front door and was making it quite clear she had no intention of moving for either man or beast. Just inside the door there was a crowd of old men, all wearing a motley collection of hats, sitting around a table playing cards. They seemed to be taking part in a scowling competition, especially if someone walked in through the door and, like me, didn't shut it quickly enough. I smiled back at them. They could scowl at me all they liked, I didn't mind climbing over sheep and I didn't mind scowling card players with singular tastes in headwear because reaching Tan Hill marked the halfway point of the Pennine Way. I headed for the bar.

Not long after I'd sat down with my beer a coachload of pensioners arrived. They were a cheerful crowd. They all ordered soup and mugs of tea instead of beer and went around the walls studying the old black and white photos of Tan Hill in bygone days when it had been cut off from the outside world by massive winter snowdrifts.

It wasn't an easy job to drag myself away from the warm fug in the bar and to get going again. And when I got outside and into the wind and rain, the afternoon's walk over Clay Hill and Washfold Rigg turned out to be as wet underfoot as anywhere I'd encountered on the walk so far, and not a single slab or paving stone in sight. So I was in for a spot of bog-trotting.

The early pioneers of walking in the Peak District and Pennines were known as bog-trotters because they spent so much of their time floundering through peat bogs. The idea involves trying to make the best progress you can while putting as little weight down on the ground as possible and in this respect it has much in common with the Natural Law Party's ideas on yogic flying. So a skilled bog-trotter covers the ground at something between a jog and a walk; the technique involves a jerky motion, sharply twitching up alternate elbows and knees, something like an ungainly dressage horse. From a distance a bog-trotter looks a bit like a marionette being worked by a particularly cack-handed puppeteer and they probably sink into the bogs every bit as much as if they had just ploughed on through the mire in the usual way.

The path on the ground wasn't very clear amongst the peat and the heather and route-finding involved following a line of white-topped stakes which had been driven into the ground. This should have been easy but some of the stakes had fallen over and some were missing altogether. A couple of times I veered wildly off track to reach a stake only to find when I got there that, by some trick of perspective, it was just a thin white wand, not much thicker than a chunky garden cane, which was marking what looked like a grouse feeding station.

Just beyond Bog Tarn, Skitter Hill and Bog Scar (I'm not making these names up, honest) and around Trough Heads the Pennine Way splits into two. The original route goes on a more northerly course through Baldersdale, but accommodation is a bit thin on the ground that way – there is Baldersdale Youth Hostel and not much else – so the Bowes Loop was created, an official alternative which swings to the east and through the village of Bowes, where there is a bit more chance of finding somewhere to stay. I was booked in at the pub, the Ancient Unicorn, a sixteenth-century coaching inn where, according to Tony from Keld Lodge (who used to be the landlord there), Charles Dickens had once dropped in for a pie and a pint.

I had expected Bowes to be bigger, a small town maybe. Instead I found a village built of grey stone with a quiet main street where most of the through traffic was diverted past on the A66. In Bowes churchyard I searched for, but failed to find, the grave of George Ashton Taylor, a schoolboy who died at Bowes Academy when it was run by the cruel headmaster William Shaw. After a visit in 1838, Dickens is said to have based the school in *Nicholas Nickleby* on Bowes Academy, and the ill-fated George Ashton Taylor formed the basis for his character Smike.

Just off the main street stood what was left of Bowes Castle, sacked and left in ruins after Robert the Bruce lay siege to it in 1322. For the first time the Scottish border didn't seem so very far away, not if Bowes Castle, or what was left of it, was once part of the defences against the marauding Scots.

Pennine Way signs were a bit thin on the ground next morning around the Bowes Loop so I was in for a bit of proper navigation. Juggling a map and compass I tried to find my way over a series of low ridges, past Hagworm Hall, (if J K Rowling hasn't put this into the latest Harry Potter I really think she should), and on to Middleton-in-Teesdale. I'd made an early start partly because I knew I had a long day ahead and also because I'd spent a pretty restless night with turbulent dreams of my own unhappy school days. I was fighting off Robert the Bruce and Scottish raiding parties till three in the morning, then Charles Dickens turned up and demanded a pint of best bitter, a pork pie and to see my history homework.

As I walked up the hill above Grassholme Farm I noticed, just protruding over the top of the ridge, a pair of knees covered with patched and faded denim. Not the usual sight on a Pennine hillside so I decided to approach with some caution. As I crested the hill I found that the knees belonged to a bald-headed chap who was stretched out on the ground by a half-built dry stonewall. I'd scoured the pages of some of the most thorough and detailed hillwalking and mountaineering manuals but none, not even under the sections on 'Dealing with Emergencies in the Hills' had ever covered this eventuality. I mentally ran through the emergency equipment packed in my rucksack – six aspirins, a safety pin and a couple of elastoplasts – and then tried to remember the procedure if someone faints or collapses. I approached a bit closer and could hear the stentorian tones of hearty snoring. Not a medical emergency after all, just a drystone waller having a nap after lunch with his tools and empty lunchbox scattered around him. I climbed over the stile as quietly as I could and moved on. He never stirred. I don't suppose he even knew I'd been past.

I made a short detour into Middleton-in-Teesdale for a cup of tea, passing the auction mart, where, from the singsong voice of the auctioneer, it seemed a sheep sale was underway. Then I was back on route and following the River Tees for the afternoon.

I'd been looking forward to this stretch of the walk and I wasn't disappointed. The sun was out, the flowers were in bloom and the sheep were in their pasture. In short it was a perfect walk alongside the water, stopping now and then to watch the little dippers perched on the stones midstream. With their dark backs, white breasts and bobbing up and down motion, dippers are often said to resemble tiny, and rather obliging, waiters, who have just taken your order for a round of exotic cocktails.

The upper Tees must be Britain's best river for waterfalls. First there is Low Force, an impressive cataract of water by most rivers' standards but for the Tees just the appetiser. The main course comes a mile or so upstream in the form of High Force, England's biggest waterfall. This is no narrow dribble of water like most apologies for a waterfall in England, at High Force the whole of the river (and the Tees is a substantial river at this point) drops in a block of foaming, rushing water down a huge step into a pool below, thundering and throwing up a cloud of spray. I'd have to wait until the next day for my pudding, Cauldon Snout, the final fall on the Tees.

As I stood watching the waters thunder over High Force and trying, and failing, to capture something of its power with my camera, an elderly chap came and stood beside me. He wore a checked shirt with a woollen tie and a greasy cap which was perched on an unruly tangle of hair. He leaned on a shepherd's crook looking out over the falls with an expression of rapture on his face.

'Wonderful, isn't it?' he said, turning and grinning at me. 'I've been at Middleton-in-Teesdale all day buying sheep and afterwards I always make a little pilgrimage up here to take a look at High Force.'

Sheep were on my mind a bit later that evening. I was cutting through a small paddock, the light was fading and I think I may have gone adrift from the path slightly. The paddock held what at first sight seemed to be a few nice woolly sheep, but on closer inspection, and when I'd reached the middle of the field, and was beyond comfortable sprinting distance from the stile, I realised that they were not just nice woolly sheep but a dozen no nonsense Swaledale Rams, with solid muscle under their fleeces and each one sporting a set of curly horns like the drop handlebars on a racing bike. Forming a rough circle they surrounded me, clearly not at all happy about having their evening disturbed by some clumsy-footed rambler. If they had worked together and come up with a coordinated strategy for dealing with lost, and by this time, frankly weary Pennine Way walkers, I could have been in serious trouble but they suffered from leadership issues. While the two in front pawed the ground with their hooves, lowered their heads and advanced with their solid-looking horns in a purposeful manner, a private scrap broke out amongst three of the rams at the rear. This made a break in the ranks wide enough for me to be able to nip through and head for the fence. The two guys leading the frontal assault became sidetracked, quarrelled amongst themselves then got mixed up in the general punch-up. Then all of the others decided to join in and while they were busy debating matters in the only way that rams know how, I managed to scramble over the fence. The way the wire had been squashed down made me think that I might not have been the first Pennine Way walker to have made a hasty escape that way.

The Cross Fell Curry House

Cauldon Snout is the third in the trilogy of waterfalls on the Upper Tees, and the one that you can't avoid getting up close and personal with. The river flows out of Cow Green Reservoir and becomes a wild cataract where it cascades down a very steep escarpment. The path hugs the right bank so closely that I was soaked by the spray before I managed to scramble to the top.

Once over the Pennine watershed I arrived at High Cup Nick. This must rank as the most unsung highlight of the Pennine Way. A deep V-shaped cleft cut into the hillside with steep crags around the rim running into scree slopes below. It looks as if a giant axe had been driven into the hillside, then wrenched out to leave a deep scar.

The walk from Dufton next day, where I'd stayed at the youth hostel, over Cross Fell to Alston is another of the Pennine Way's epic days. I was lucky again with the weather. The walk starts with a pleasant stroll through the valley along some shady lanes and then the climbing begins in earnest with a long pull up Green Fell, Knock Fell and onto the summit of Great Dun Fell, which is covered with all kinds of Ministry of Defence techno stuff. I took a break there and sat in the shade of what looked like a giant golf ball before tackling the big one, Cross Fell, the highest point of the Pennine Way (all 893 metres of it) and the highest point of the End to End so far.

I reached the summit of Cross Fell at 2.05pm and had just patted the trig point when a chubby, red-faced man popped up from behind a pile of rocks. He asked me if I could point him to the alterative route down to Kirkland. As I wasn't at all sure where Kirkland was I got the map out.

'Oh, that's a good idea,' said the red-faced man. 'Somehow I never got it together to bring a map with me.'

As it happened my map wasn't a lot of use to him because it was one of the Pennine Way strip maps and Kirkland wasn't on it.

'I suppose I'll just have to go back the way I came up,' he said.

'Good idea,' I said, although I did feel just little bit bad about not being able to help him much, fellowship on the hills and all that, but really I didn't know where Kirkland was, it wasn't on my map and I had to press on if I was going to get to Alston before dark. Then, as if it was divine intervention for leaving him to his own devices, I couldn't find the path from the summit to get down to Garrigill.

The top of Cross Fell forms a large dome, almost a plateau, mostly made up of uneven boulders with no obvious path. I took a compass bearing and tried to follow the cairns but they seemed a bit random so I floundered around for a bit in bog, amongst the heather and then through a boulder field until eventually I came across the bridle track to Garrigill more by luck than by judgement. After half a mile I found a signpost for Kirkland and when, another half mile further on, I bumped into my red-faced, map-less pal again I was able to show him where we were on my map and point him in the right direction for Kirkland and so I didn't feel too bad after all.

It was good track down to Garrigill, a long slow descent which contoured around the hill but very stony underfoot and tough on the feet. I knew I still had a long way to go and felt under a time pressure, which was a great shame because it was superb open moorland, the weather was warm and sunny and it would have been great to have had a bit more time to stop and to just take in my surroundings.

Garrigill was bathed in a soft, warm evening light when I reached it, a charming cluster of stone cottages set around a village green. By this time my legs were starting to go into something of a revolt. They were telling me in no uncertain terms that it was time to stop, and my feet were egging them on. Common sense said stop, but my itinerary said no, you've still got another four miles to go before you reach Alston. When I was planning this stage I'd lingered for a long time over the Garrigill B&Bs in my accommodation guide before deciding how another few miles to Alston wouldn't be a problem. Across the road I watched two cyclists getting off their bikes and knocking on the door of what seemed to be a cosy and welcoming B&B. I saw the door being opened by a motherly-looking woman who stood wiping her hands on her apron.

'Oh, yes,' I heard one of the cyclists say. 'We've had a really long day.'

'Aye,' said the second one. 'I'm fair done in.'

They looked as fresh as daisies to me.

'Can't wait to put my feet up,' said the first.

'You poor dears,' said the motherly-looking woman. 'I'll put the kettle on and make you a cup of tea.'

I coaxed my aching legs to start moving again and tried not to think about the cyclists with their feet up drinking tea.

I reached Alston Youth Hostel at 6.40pm and with my last scraps of energy I made up my bed, had a shower and tried to make myself presentable, and then I set off into the now darkened town of Alston, to try and find something to eat.

Like most End to End walkers I seemed to live mostly on pub grub so I rolled into the pub, the one recommended by the youth hostel warden as serving good food. I ordered a pint of their guest beer and started to peruse the bar food menu.

'We're a bit busy tonight,' said the barman as he handed me my beer.

'Never mind,' I said, 'I can always have another pint while I'm waiting.'

'Well we've got a party in, see?'

'The steak and ale pie sounds good.'

'I mean it might be a little while before we can serve you.'

'Does it come with chips and gravy?'

'Like,' he said, 'it might be quicker if you tried somewhere else.'

'I don't mind waiting,' I said, 'couldn't walk another step.'

'What I mean is ...' And at this point he snatched the menu clean out of my hand. 'We've got a party in, all wanting food, and if I walk into the kitchen now with another order the chef will throw a meat cleaver at me so you'll just have to go somewhere else.'

Alston claims to be the highest town in England and it has one of the steepest main streets which my post-Cross Fell legs didn't appreciate one bit. The town seemed sunk in a gloom of gritty post-industrial northern decline as I walked its deserted cobbles. The second pub I tried didn't do food at all. The next one didn't do food on Thursdays or only when Saturn is aligned with Jupiter, I can't remember which. Finally I found one of those strange hybrid curry house pubs which seem to be springing up everywhere. In the main bar *Coronation Street* was blasting out of the TV and there was no real ale on hand pumps but at least they did do food; assuming you like curry that is, and nothing but curry. They served me up a chicken Madras with all the trimmings and in double quick time. It was the most amazing disappearing curry. I could remember picking my fork up then, in what seemed like the blinking of an eye, my plate was empty and I was mopping up the final drops of sauce with the last of my garlic and coriander nan.

The effects of a good meal, not only on my stomach and on my legs, but also on my general world view, was wondrous to behold. Alston no longer seemed sunk in a post-industrial gloom, it became a haven brimming with northern country charm. The sort of place where you might expect to see all the women wearing bonnets, shawls and aprons, and all the men kitted out in waistcoats and cloth caps. Or where you might find yourself dodging parties of clog dancers and black pudding makers while a brass band plays brightly in the background. I felt so good I even decided to forgive the first pub and call back there for a last pint on the way home.

'Hello again,' said the barman, obviously noting my new

chirpy disposition. 'You found something to eat then?'

In Granny's Room
After the comparative isolation of Cross Fell, Hadrian's
Wall on a Saturday morning felt like taking a hike along a
main street. There were walkers everywhere. Some were
exploring the ruins of Thirlwall Castle, some were
following the Geology Trail and some, a rambling club
from Newcastle, I think, were making very little headway
at all because one of their number was clearly having
trouble with his boots. From what I could gather, bits kept
falling off first one boot, then the other, which had
prompted a bit of path-side cobbling. I met an elderly
couple from Sussex who were walking Hadrian's Wall to
get in training for a trek to Nepal with their grandson. The
granddad took me to one side and asked me if I thought
there would be a lot of steep steps in Nepal. 'It's my knees,'
he said. 'They're not what they were.'

I fell in with a couple from Northampton and walked
with them for a few miles while they quizzed me about my
walk so far, and then the rain started sluicing down and
suddenly all the weekenders and wall walkers disappeared
and I had Hadrian's best known legacy all to myself.

The Wall runs along the top of an escarpment which,
from the northern side, must have formed a formidable
barrier to the marauding Scots. It also made for some
unexpectedly strenuous walking. I'd planned a short day's
walk, about six miles, and was considering it to be
something of a rest day. I don't know what I'd been
expecting, rolling hills maybe, gentle fields, stopping off
now and again to indulge in a little field study around some
of the more notable Roman remains. I hadn't bargained on
steep and precipitous gradients.

Sweating inside my waterproofs, I laboured up banks at such crazy angles my nose, bloodhound-like, was just inches from the muddy path. Then, like a roller coaster, I was down the other side before the next steep uphill. It was like being back on the Cornish coast path. The mist had closed in and visibility was down to a few yards. I felt as if I was walking in a bubble isolating me from the rest of the world. There was just the Wall, the rain, the mud and me. A runner wearing a florescent green woolly hat overtook me at some speed then quickly vanished into the mist, his florescent hat being the last bit of him to disappear. It bobbed around like a will-o-the-wisp before it too was absorbed by the gathering gloom.

By the time I reached the trigpoint on Winshields Crag the weather was beginning to clear a bit and when I came out onto the road at the Steel Riggs car park I decided that an excursion down to the visitor centre at Once Brewed might be in order. I thought it might give me a chance to dry out a bit and maybe get a cup of coffee.

While I was sitting in the visitor centre, steaming gently and drinking my coffee, there were at least four groups of fit-looking types, all dressed in tracksuits and trainers, who came in and asked at the accommodation desk about somewhere to stay. The lady there told them all the same, that everywhere was fully booked for miles around because the next day, a Sunday, was the Great North Run, over in Gateshead. I sat there feeling quite smug knowing that my B&B was safely booked.

Coffee finished I set off to walk back over the ridge past Steel Riggs car park and on to my B&B, which was at one of the local farms. When I passed the car park I noticed a group of walkers, all in waterproofs and carrying day sacks, climbing into a mud-spattered long wheelbase Land Rover. I walked on down the hill and found the farm where I was due to stay the night and as I was walking up the drive the Land Rover rattled past me at quite a speed then braked hard and, with a spray of gravel, came to a sudden halt in front of the farm. The driver, a woman of about forty with a frizz of grey hair and wearing a Smirnoff tee shirt, jumped out. She seemed in something of a tizz.

'Are you Mr Richards?' Her hands flapped around aimlessly in the air and her eyes didn't seem to want to meet mine. 'Oh, Mr Richards, I've been trying to phone you all day, Mr Richards, but your mobile phone's been switched off. You see we've had a terrible problem with your booking.'

'Oh dear,' I said, the implications of her words not really sinking in at first.

'You see we've got our group of Hadrian's Wall walkers.' She flapped her hand at the ramblers, all climbing out of the Land Rover at this point, clutching their rucksacks. 'And then, you see, three Great North Runners arrived and I just couldn't turn them away. Well could I?'

'Of course not,' I said, 'just so long as you didn't give them my bed, eh?'

She glanced over at the group of Hadrian's Wall walkers then her eyes flicked back towards mine but they couldn't quite make it and swerved away at the last minute. They settled for focusing somewhere over my right shoulder.

I sat down on a bench by the front door and started to take my boots off on the principle that it is unthinkable that you could move a walker on once he has removed his boots.

'Well I suppose there's Granny's room,' she said. 'We can always put you in there.'

I never did find out what they did with Granny. Her room was dark, gloomy, cave-like and full of old lady's clutter. A stale smell hung in the air which reminded me of old clothes and church jumble sales. Under the bed was a half-empty box of incontinence pads and beside them a pair of well-worn furry slippers. Above a dressing table, which was piled high with bottles of potions and pills, were some family wedding photos which, judging from the style of the clothes, must have been from circa 1970. On the far wall was a photo of the woman with the Smirnoff tee shirt back in the days when she was a slim and elfin-faced girl. She was kneeling on the grass in a garden full of roses hugging a large tabby cat.

Granny's room was also so hot it was like walking into the tropics. I tried to turn the radiator down but the valve was painted over and stuck on full. There were no windows to open so I spent a sweltering night. The only door led into a ramshackle conservatory where the dogs slept and I had to share the farm workers' bathroom. At two in the morning someone, somewhere in the house, flushed a loo which set the dogs off howling. Being a farm the household woke up at five o'clock and started preparing breakfast. Breakfast seemed to involve a lot of riveting and panel beating. And just as I was beginning to doze off again, I heard them giving the Great North Runners a hearty and rousing farewell.

The Cheviots

By this point of the walk I'd discovered that the quantity (and quality) of my note taking fluctuated in line with the weather. On a bright sunny day I'd easily slip into Wordsworthian mode and fill my notebook with musings of a lyrical and romantic nature. But when the weather closed in my notes became shorter and rather more to the point. The only thing I'd recorded for the walk from Bellingham to Byrness was 'a good day, especially if you like sphagnum moss'. After Byrness it was the Cheviots, a set of high and rounded hills just south of the border with Scotland. They are as wild and remote as anywhere in England and, if you're heading north, they are the last gasp of the Pennine Way. Their remoteness, and the general lack of anywhere to stay up there, has always presented something of a problem. There are three ways to tackle the Cheviots. You can go for broke and do them in one mammoth twenty-six-mile hike. You can doss down in one of the two mountain refuges which are up there, or you can do as I did and take a diversion a mile or two off route and find one of the odd remote farms which were still doing bed and breakfast.

From Byrness it was a steep climb up through the forest then out along an open ridge where a brisk wind was blowing and doing a good job of keeping the rain at bay. There was nothing on the ground to show where the border with Scotland was but by my reckoning I crossed into Scotland around midday up by Coquet Head. I did feel that a gathering of the massed band of pipes and drums would have been in order or at the very least a guard of honour from the Argyle and Sutherland Highlanders but instead I had to settle for just sitting down on a tuft of heather and treating myself to the Kit Kat I'd found in the top pocket of my rucksack, which must have been lurking in there since before Alston. Deep down I did feel something of a glow to think I'd walked the entire length of England. Then, as soon as I'd finished my Kit Kat the path crossed straight back into England so it was pretty short-lived as glows of satisfaction went. The Pennine Way flirts with the Scottish border through most of the Cheviots and I wouldn't cross into Scotland for good until the following day.

Just before I reached Yearning Saddle, the first of the mountain refuges, I watched as five walkers emerged from it blinking in the sunlight. They were the first walkers I'd seen since the Roman wall and I greeted them like long-lost friends. They, on the other hand, seemed less inclined to chat. They said they were running late and were keen to press on to Byrness.

I took a peek inside the refuge. It was a sturdily-built structure with a substantial bench around three of the walls which would be wide enough to sleep on, a shovel (if I could have got a signal I'd have phoned Anna) and even a sleeping bag hanging up on a line. On the shelves were odd bits and pieces that had been left by previous visitors, things which a stranded walker might just find useful: a tin opener, a stub of candle, a damp box of matches and a couple of quite ancient dehydrated packet meals.

A mile or so beyond the refuge I came across two soldiers in full battle kit taking a nap in the heather. Their field craft must have been a bit suspect because they had chosen the most exposed spot they could find to set up a bivi tent, then they'd just kipped down beside it with their assault rifles for company. They nearly jumped out of their camouflage when I walked up behind them and said hello. Maybe they thought I was their C.O. (maybe I was lucky not to get shot).

At West Cairn Hill I followed the spur off the main route on a boggy path to the summit of the Cheviot itself. This wasn't strictly necessary but it seemed a shame to be up there and not go to the top. On the summit I met three Geordies with a greyhound sitting in the shelter of the cairn and eating bananas. They asked me if I thought the Pennine Way was a good route. I said I'd recommend it.

Then it was back to the main drag and on to The Schil, which is the last substantial hill of the Cheviots. Shortly after that I crossed the border into Scotland for the last time (yippee!). Then there was a long descent to join the road a mile or so before Kirk Yetholm. Even this short stretch of road starts off uphill before it finally relents and drops down into Kirk Yetholm itself. I touched base at the Border Hotel and then went inside to raise a glass to Pennine Bitter Men (and women) all, wherever they may be.

At the bar I sat next to a local chap who was wearing a proper Scottish bonnet on his head and had a small dog sitting beside him tethered to the bar stool by a length of knotted string. I took my phone out to call home and boast, just a little bit, about having done the Pennine Way, but I couldn't get a signal and the pub didn't have a payphone. The man with the dog took pity on me.

'Ach, nay problem,' he said. He dug his hand into the pocket of his fleece and handed me his mobile. 'Use mine, I've loads of free minutes.'

I was already starting to look forward to my walk up through Scotland.

PART THREE – THE DEEP NORTH AND THE ROAD TO HELL

The Mighty Deerstalker

The crack of a shotgun going off was close enough to leave my ears ringing. Then I heard the pellets rattle in the hazel branches not very far above my head. They couldn't be shooting at me, could they? Shotgun barrel number two went off with just as loud a report seconds later, but this time I didn't hear the pellets in the trees. And there was a very good reason why I didn't hear the rattle of the pellets; by that time I'd already stuffed my thermos flask into my rucksack, hauled my pack on my back and was off and away down the track faster than any Olympic sprinter has ever made it out of the starting blocks. I wasn't going to give whoever it was out there toting the heavy artillery the chance to reload and have another go. Before he was primed, loaded and ready to pull the trigger again I intended to be nothing more than a dot on the horizon and disappearing fast.

I was just a little way north of Kelso and whether I was trespassing or not was, I suppose, something of a moot point. As far as most End to Enders would have been concerned I was way off route again. Kelso does not usually figure on the typical End to End itinerary. A more logical approach would have been to strike off from somewhere in the middle of the Cheviots, head for Jedburgh then follow the Southern Uplands Way as it heads north towards Peebles. I, on the other hand, with memories of the Pennine Bitter Men to the fore, had decided I wanted to walk the whole Pennine Way, which took me through to Kirk Yetholm and further east than I really wanted to be. From Kirk Yetholm it was a short hop to Kelso, where I took a break from End to Ending for the winter. With the first shoots of spring (no pun intended) I was back on route again and picking my way, cross country on a mish-mash of paths, tracks and back roads, aiming firstly to dodge any volleys of shotgun pellets which happened to be fired off in my direction, secondly for the town of Melrose and thirdly for Peebles and something like a proper north-south End to End route again. I was looking forward to Peebles, a town where, for reasons I'd been unable to fathom, I had not been able to book any accommodation at all. Although, what on earth could be happening there to make it so popular at the back end of March, I really couldn't imagine.

If most End to End walkers give Kelso the elbow then all I can say is that it's their loss. Kelso, with its grand market square and ruined abbey, is a charming Border town. It stands at the confluence of the Rivers Tweed and Teviot, and has some of the best salmon fishing in the country. This might account for why every other shop on the high street is a fishing tackle shop. And it was in one of these emporiums of piscatorial pleasure that they had a calendar displayed in the window: 'Women in Waders'. It depicted a young lady wearing little more than a pair of green thigh-length waders, her rather obvious assets being barely concealed by the rather large salmon she was holding. I dragged myself away strong-mindedly. Such images are apt to prey on the mind of the solitary walker and anyway it was high time to set off and get back to some serious End to Ending.

I started out on the Border Abbey's Way and along the

banks of the River Teviot through to Roxburgh, amid blue skies and a brisk wind which was strong enough to make me stop and pull my cagoule on before I'd even left town. At Rutherford Mains I found a disused railway track which would avoid a section of the A699. The track heading east back towards Roxburgh was surfaced, signposted and was clearly well used. The track west ran behind a line of cottages and was overgrown with brambles, stunted trees and birch poles. Underfoot it was soft and loamy. There were prints showing that a horse had been along there recently but not many walkers. As the morning was getting on and it was the first day out I decided a short elevenses break was in order. I'd found a sheltered spot in a hazel thicket and had just poured myself a cup of coffee out of my flask when the unofficial Rambo of Roxburgh whipped out his twelve bore and started peppering the landscape all around with buckshot.

The afternoon was less eventful, in that nobody took pot shots at me, and I was able to stroll along the banks of the Tweed in one piece. But other hazards awaited in the Eildon Hills, hazards of a more supernatural nature. I made a stop by the Rhymer's Stone. The spot where, according to legend, Thomas the Rhymer had dozed off one day under a tree and woken up to find he'd been whisked away to Elfland, where he was held prisoner by the Fairy Queen for seven years. I was feeling a bit weary myself by this point and the thought of taking my rucksack off, laying down and having a nap was very tempting, but no, seven years in Elfland would play havoc with my schedule. However, there may be compensations, if maybe the Fairy Queen had a pair of green thigh-length waders ...

It could be that I was still unfit after my winter layoff but, next morning when I set out from Melrose in the rain, my rucksack felt particularly heavy. With the water dripping off the front of my hood, grey skies and nothing much to look at, as I was walking along I found myself ticking off a sort of mental inventory of everything I had onboard. I had packed an extra fleece, but it was March and I could easily come across snow on the higher ground. There was a flask of coffee. I didn't mind swigging cold tap water during the summer months but in the bad weather a mug of hot coffee could be a great morale booster. It was then that the thought hit me. There was one very important item of equipment which I'd carried with me on all previous stages of the walk, but, after my winter layoff I'd simply forgotten to pack. I felt so stupid. I was supposed to be an experienced walker for heaven's sake, and here I was, nearly two thirds of the way through, how could I leave something so important at home at this late stage in the proceedings? I suppose I'd become too complacent and maybe just a little bit lax when it came to packing, but I'd bawl anybody else out for forgetting such an essential bit of kit. Well I hadn't got it, so I'd just have to manage without. Maybe I could buy one when I reached Peebles.

A mile or two short of Innerleithen I came across the first of the fun-runners. A group of five girls skidded down a steep bank at the side of the road and bounced off the scrim netting which had been set up at the bottom. Two girls were dressed as clowns, another as a scuba diver with a mask and snorkel, one as a Barbie doll and one as a teddy bear. They were spattered with mud but in high spirits and waved at me as they jogged past.

Innerleithen itself, when I arrived, was swarming with runners who all seemed to be taking their task rather more seriously. They certainly didn't want to stop or hang about for a chat. Some had already finished their race and there was a lot of swaggering about going on, showing off the medals dangling around their necks. By the time I reached Traquair House and peered in through the gates I could see the place was heaving. There were tents, stalls, marquees and tinny Highland music being played over loudspeakers mounted on top of tall poles.

I asked a chap wearing a high visibility jacket who was standing outside the gate directing traffic what was going on. 'Aye,' he said, turning his attention away from the traffic and looking at me with a pair of sad eyes. ''Tis the *Mighty* Deerstalker. Aye, competitive mountain runs of five and ten kilometres. Up over yon hill and down into the dale, a mighty race, mighty and tough.' He looked me up and down. 'And only for the *fittest* of mountain men.'

It gave me a sort of glow really, to know that I hadn't lost my touch. I could still blunder into major sporting events anywhere in the country with total and blissful ignorance. It also explained why all the hotels and B&Bs in Peebles were full, and why I was having to stay at a golf spa resort out of town which was costing me an arm and a leg.

Next morning, while all the Mighty Deerstalkers were still slumbering, I made an early start to walk into town, anxious to replace my vital bit of missing equipment. But it was Sunday, and in that corner of Scotland they are still very keen on keeping the Sabbath. All the shops in Peebles were shut.

The Pentlands

'So are you going all the way to John O'Groats then?'

I was just a bit taken aback to be asked this by the landlady at the B&B in West Linton. As far as I was concerned John O'Groats was still a very long way off and

I still hadn't started freely admitting to anyone yet that it was my ultimate destination. It still felt too much like tempting fate. But I shouldn't really have been surprised, End to Enders are about the only visitors West Linton gets because it makes a convenient halt between Peebles and Edinburgh. The landlady also put me right on my pronunciation of Milngavie, which is where the West Highland Way starts. It should be pronounced *Mull-guy*.

I'd walked over the previous day from Peebles following the Old Drovers' Road. These routes, where cattle would be walked over the hills from the Highlands and on to the markets in town, are a feature in Scotland. The drovers, whose job it was to drive the cattle along, were a wild and hardy bunch of characters who would doss down in the heather at nights next to their cattle, with only their plaids and a nip of whisky to keep out the cold. The path from Peebles to West Linton wasn't marked as a drove road on my map but after I chanced on a sign for it by the outskirts of town I decided to take a risk and follow it over the hill to West Linton. It was a good walk and, incidentally, I managed fine without my vital piece of equipment.

I was making for Edinburgh, via the Pentland Hills. It looked like it was going to be a long day and the forecast was bad. Opposite the pub, the Gordon Arms, I followed a lane called The Loan which joined the Roman road to Carlops after about a mile. Beyond Carlops there was a bend in the road at Nine Mile Burn where the path branched off into the Pentland Hills. The rain, which had been threatening all morning, started, first with big sleety drops before setting in to become persistent and icy. The wind was blowing in increasingly strong gusts and the mist had started to drift in and was already beginning to obscure the tops of the hills. In conditions like these the prudent hillwalker would, of course, reach for that most vital piece of navigational equipment, a compass. And I knew exactly where to put my hand on my compass, it was nestling at the bottom of the second drawer down in my desk at home.

So if I didn't have my compass; I'd been careless enough to leave it behind when I'd set out on this first Scottish leg after my winter break. I'd just have to manage without it, at least until I reached Edinburgh, where there should be camping shops and I could buy a replacement. In the meantime I was faced with something of a dilemma: to try to cross the Pentland Hills in deteriorating weather with a map but no compass, or walk thirteen miles along the busy A702 with no footpath for most of the way. The answer was never really in any doubt. I climbed over the stile and headed for the hills.

So sans compass I set off into the mist. The path was easy to follow at first. Just below Monk Rig I surprised a flock of at least a dozen curlews sheltering in the lee of a stone wall. Startled, they laboured into the air for ten feet until they reached a point where the full force of the gale caught them, then they turned, and in a synchronised manoeuvre they sped away downwind like a squadron of jet fighters.

I climbed higher until I crested the hill, where I caught a gust of wind so strong it made me stagger sideways. This was the moment when the rain cover on my backpack chose to take on all the properties of a racing yacht's spinnaker. It hoisted itself aloft, inflated, hove to, cast itself adrift from my rucksack and, like a square rigger on the larboard tack, set sail for the Firth of Forth. Well it would have done if I hadn't, on this occasion, remembered to tie it on with a length of bungee cord. So it sprang back with a twang when it reached the extent of the elasticity of the bungee, quite spoiling the nautical effect, then it flapped around in the wind like a soggy black flag and started to tangle itself around the rucksack straps so I had to spend an undignified ten minutes on my hands and knees in the peat, mud and rain trying to fix it back on again.

As the visibility deteriorated and the hills receded into the mist I became isolated in a grey world where nothing seemed real except the grass, the cold and the wet. Up ahead through the gloom I thought I could just discern something moving. It looked as if there was something out there: something, or somebody, lurking. Something that was not rain or sleet, or rock or heather. Something that was flesh and blood and muscle and sinew. It was out there and it was squarely blocking my path, hiding in the fog, a hunched form, indistinct yet bulky, shape-shifting and massive. I strained my eyes into the gloom and it seemed to dissolve and then reform, the one became many. I was wet and I was cold, alone, not at all sure where I was and hopelessly outnumbered. There could be no doubt they had been waiting out there, waiting in the mist and the fog to waylay me. I could hear their snorting and stamping as they bunched up before moving in for the kill. They could only be mammoths, forgotten by history, left behind by a retreating ice age and undiscovered in this remote corner of Scotland. Then a freakish gust of wind tore the mist aside and they were revealed as half a dozen shaggy Highland cattle looking bedraggled and forlorn, standing with their backs to the wind and rain. All the same, I gave their horns a wide berth.

In the end it was the wind, the wind which had nearly stolen my pack cover, which came to my rescue. If I could just keep the wind on the left side of my face, I thought, it would keep me in a straight line and stop me from drifting off course. If it kept blowing, then I might just make it to Edinburgh. If it decided to change direction I'd be done for.

As I dropped down from Cap Law the shoulder of the hill gave me some relief, at last, from the constant battering of the wind and for the first time since Nine Mile Burn I was able to walk in a straight line. To my right I could just make out the small plantation which was marked on my map and, below West Kip, wonder of wonders, a signpost. I descended to Logan Burn, below the cloud base and out of the mist, and was soon able to pick out the shape of Threipmuir Reservoir. Then I was on a good lane and it was an easy walk all the way to Balerno, a curiously Italian sounding name, I've always thought, for a small town on the outskirts of Edinburgh.

When I hit the tarmac, I found somewhere to sit and stopped to take my gaiters off. I did this partly so I didn't look quite so mud spattered, disreputable and dishevelled when I reached town, and also to get some breeze around my legs. It always made me feel a bit like a footballer whenever I did this. A footballer playing extra time in the FA Cup Final, who rolls down his stockings to let the air get to tired calf muscles. Extra time in my case was a seemingly endless trek, first alongside the river, the Water of Leith, and then along the towpath of the Union Canal and into Edinburgh.

It was late afternoon and the towpath into the city was thronged with joggers, cyclists and office workers all heading for home. There were even some school children sculling along the canal in a racing boat while their gym teacher, muffled up in scarves and jumpers, cycled along the bank yelling out orders through a megaphone. Even though it was the end of the day everyone seemed fit, healthy and bursting with energy whereas I, by this time, was reduced to a geriatric shuffle. I'd covered seventy-five miles in four days and I was feeling every inch of it.

I finally left the canal and made my way into the city looking for a landmark, any landmark, I might recognise.

'CAN I INTEREST YOU ... IN THE *BIG* ... *ISSUE*?' For a small man he had an exceptionally loud voice. He stood by the statue of that most faithful of dogs, Greyfriars Bobby, on the corner of Candlemaker Row and seemed quite oblivious to the rain. His copies of the *Big Issue* were wrapped in plastic to protect them from the weather but he looked even wetter than me, if that were possible. His dark hair was plastered to his head and hung in rattails over his collar. His glasses were misted and he peered myopically through them. The Edinburgh workers, intent on home, swarmed past ignoring him. As I passed he said, 'You look as if you've been on a country walk, sir.'

'Yes,' I said, 'I suppose I have.'

'Copy of the *Big Issue*?'

'Sorry,' I said, knowing all of my small change was packed deep in my rucksack. He looked suddenly depressed and wetter than ever.

'CAN I INTEREST YOU ... IN THE *BIG* ... *ISSUE*. COUNTRY WALKING EDITION?'

'Well okay then.' I fumbled under the wet pack cover to find some change.

Slowly and painfully I entered the city, found a small backstreet hotel, went up to my room, sat down, took my boots off and then just sat there. I didn't even have the energy to go downstairs to the bar.

Next morning, after a good night's sleep and an even better breakfast, feeling somewhat recovered, I went out into the City of Edinburgh, found an outdoors shop and bought myself a shiny new compass.

Broken on the Wheel

It didn't seem quite right somehow, not considering how Scotland is famous for its hills and mountains, to be setting out to walk from Edinburgh to the outskirts of Glasgow and not be climbing a single hill, fell or even a bump in the ground that was worth the name. But what End to End walker could pass on such an obvious and ready-made route? Didn't I dream of smooth, even, level tracks, and all of them free of traffic? Well now I had my wish. I could follow the towpaths of, first the Union Canal, and then the Forth and Clyde Canal, and swan my way into Glasgow without even breaking a sweat. Well that was the theory. It was beginning to sound something like End to End walker heaven. Not only would I be walking there on the flat, the Union Canal from Edinburgh to just beyond Falkirk sticks to the 73-metre contour all the way. It doesn't have a single lock until the Falkirk Wheel and it doesn't rise or fall one iota. What it lacks in the lock department it makes up for in distance, by snaking its way all around the county for mile after redundant mile to avoid any changes of level.

I'd had a rest day in Edinburgh and, while I wasn't quite stepping out with a spring in my step, my progress back out of the city was a bit more sprightly than it had been on the way in. The canal went through a seemingly endless urban sprawl: houses, square blocks of flats, sudden green spaces and nursery schools with names like 'Pixies' or 'Little Rascals' picked out in multicoloured letters. When I reached the edge of town the houses were replaced by ploughed fields. It was too early for the crops to have sprouted so they were mostly just bare earth. The hedgerows had not come to life yet, and the trees were still without leaves. Pleasant, rural, if unremarkable, scenery, but this was Scotland's industrial belt so I for one wasn't complaining.

The stretch from Broxburn through to Winchburn was a bit more industrial and a bit more built-up, where the back garden fences of council houses reached down to the towpath. Not picturesque maybe but I'd certainly been through far worse on the walk. And to add a bit of interest, there were some curious red slagheaps along the canal bank, but these heaps didn't go to the usual point, their summits were flattened, as if they had been sliced away, like the top of a hard boiled-egg. Then beyond Winchburn it was back to the country, not that I could see much of the countryside because the canal went into a deep cutting lined with trees which, even though they were still leafless, were packed so tightly together they managed to shut out most of the light. Then a thin drizzle of rain started and I began to feel I was locked into my own world of half light and dripping trees.

I was surprised how few people were using the towpath. I'd seen three pike fishermen earlier, sitting gloomily over their rods – they didn't even look up as I went past – and just before Broxburn I'd stopped to chat to a man who had taken the back wheel off his bike and was busy repairing a puncture. He seemed incredibly chipper about it and positively gleeful, a quarter of an hour later, when he cycled silently up behind me then started frantically ringing his bell. I was deep in my own thoughts and nearly jumped out of my waterproofs while he rode away laughing so much I thought for a minute he would wobble into the canal.

I had started the morning feeling I was walking well but by mid-afternoon the distance and the monotony was beginning to wear me down. There were no distractions, no boats and the towpath was quite empty. There was just me, the rain and the leafless, dripping trees. The temperature dropped another notch and the afternoon light became cold, grey and flat, which more or less summed up my mood. My legs became stiff and chilled through; they just didn't want to move any more. The optimism of the morning had evaporated and was replaced with gloom and drizzle. I shouldn't be feeling like this, I kept trying to tell myself. If I was slogging through peat bogs I could moan. If I was struggling up steep, slippery mountainsides I might have cause to grumble but here I was on a good smooth path that was spirit-level flat. And nobody was making me do it. I was there of my own free will. I was retired, a gentleman of leisure. I could have been at home, if I had wanted to be, couch-bound, feet up and in front of the telly. I wasn't really complaining, it was just that it shouldn't have been so painful, not that late on in the walk.

As it turned out, the twenty-four miles from Edinburgh to Linlithgow, along the canal, was the longest day of the trip so far and, when it came to totting up all of the distances with the aid of my little orange map measurer friend, I discovered it was the longest day's walk of the entire End to End. I also rubbed the third (and last) blister of the walk as I trudged along the canal (the second blister had been much earlier, on the road between Burton and Derby). As a walk Edinburgh to Linlithgow was even further than I'd planned, and further than I'd originally measured on the map because somehow I managed to book a hotel that was not only out of town, but out of town and at the top of the only hill for miles (hooray for internet booking!).

The local population seemed to use the canal as a dumping ground. It was always easy to tell when I was nearing a centre of population because there was a lot more rubbish in the canal, and a lot more dog muck on the towpath. There were empty pop bottles floating upside down, a surprising amount of quite serviceable-looking footballs, usually just tantalisingly out of reach from the bank, and, not far from Park Farm a decent set of five-a-side goal posts, with the nets still attached.

By mid-afternoon of day two on the towpath, I doubt that I had met half a dozen people all day. There had been a jogger or two and a dog walker around Redding but that was about it. A thin rain started at two o'clock and the canal ran into a narrow tree-lined cutting which shut out what little light was managing to struggle through the thick grey clouds. I had seen nobody for hours. I wasn't sure where I was. I knew I wasn't lost. Just as long as I had the canal on my left I couldn't get lost, but I had no idea how far I'd come or how far I had to go. The deep trough seemed as if it was a world apart, a lonely world, uninhabited by birds, animals or people. I supposed there would be fish swimming in the depths of the cold green water but they seemed to offer little by way of comfort and apart from the pale belly of a dead perch floating upside down in the reeds I never saw any fish along the entire length of the canal.

Up ahead I saw a bench of black wrought iron, beaded with raindrops and with an engraved plaque attached to the back. A cheerless place for a bench maybe, but I thought a short break would be in order. A cup of coffee from my flask would lift the spirits and go down a treat. I slipped my rucksack off and had to squint to read the inscription in the poor light. The bench was dedicated to a man who had, one day, dropped dead at this spot. I put my rucksack back on again; coffee could wait.

Although I'd been expecting it, when I rounded the bend and saw the dark opening of the Falkirk Tunnel it came as a shock. A sign stated that it was 620 metres long. The gaping entrance was like a toothless mouth frozen mid-scream. My feet stopped, apparently of their own accord. I felt suddenly reluctant. I edged forward and peered inside. There was the sound of water dripping incessantly from the roof and plopping into the canal. I could just make out a pale light at the far end. It might be the proverbial light at the end of the tunnel but it looked a long way off and I didn't fancy it one bit. Once, as a teenager, I spent a night in a rambling old house with some friends and we passed the time scaring ourselves shitless telling each other ghost stories. Then there was a power cut, or some wag switched off the electricity, I can't remember which, the lights went out and we were all too frightened to go to bed. But at least I was with some mates then to have a laugh with but standing there in the drizzle at the mouth of the Falkirk Tunnel there were no friends to pull each others' leg, or to have a bit of a giggle with and to dispel the irrational fears. There was nobody, and that was the trouble. It was the loneliest place imaginable. Common sense told me there was no reason why anybody, or indeed anything, would be lurking down that miserable dark hole but it was an afternoon for primeval fears winning out over logic and common sense.

I didn't dash down the tunnel in a blind panic, honestly I didn't. But neither did I hang about. Even then it took me all of ten minutes to walk through. Ten minutes skidding around on the slippery wet cobbles, ten minutes of constant dripping water torture and ten minutes plunged into stygian gloom. There was a rail at the edge of the towpath, presumably to stop the unwary missing their step and falling into the black waters, and there were pale yellow lights fixed to the roof which seemed, if anything, to emphasise the gloom. As I reached the far end, the noise of traffic passing overhead started to drown out the sound of the water until the point where the water seemed to

187

cascade out of a drain, in a constant stream into the canal. And then I was out. Out into the fresh air and out into the rain. Never have leaden skies and persistent drizzle felt quite so welcome.

These were long days of walking. I averaged seventeen miles per day for this 'Borders' leg of the walk and I was feeling the pace. It didn't help when I looked at the map because for all the distance I was covering along the canal it was largely east to west, there was very little taking me north.

If the canal path was dreary it had one splendid highlight, the eighth wonder of the canal world, the Falkirk Wheel. It might have been a feat of engineering to build the Union Canal from Edinburgh entirely on the level and with no locks but it pales into insignificance beside the Falkirk Wheel, which is the world's only circular boat lift. A futuristic construction which made the previous ladder of eleven locks redundant as it transports barges 150 feet vertically from the Union Canal to the Forth and Clyde Canal.

To my untrained eye it didn't look anything like a wheel. It looked more like two huge grey cams rotating around a massive axle. The small boy in me is easily awoken by trains and boats and massive bits of engineering like this and I spent a happy twenty minutes, quite oblivious to the bucketing rain, watching the wheel moving narrow boats up and down. Then, with a heavy sigh, I knew I couldn't put the evil moment off any longer. I turned up my collar and headed off, out into the rain along the canal towpath. I'd swapped the Union Canal for the Forth and Clyde Canal but you could hardly tell any difference. The Forth and Clyde Canal was a bit wider and it had the occasional lock, but it was still as cold, still as wet and the bankside scenery just as featureless. If the Falkirk Wheel was the high point of the canal walk the low point was one particularly wide and exposed stretch between Banknock and Kilsyth, two and half miles long and as straight as a rod. I was walking into a stiff headwind with sleety, penetrating rain which chilled me through to the bone; it seemed to go on forever.

Just beyond Cadder, after fifty-five miles of towpath walking, and with a whoop of delight, I turned off the canal and followed a road. For ten minutes I kept glancing back over my left shoulder in sort of a reflex action to see where the water had gone. The road followed a dog-leg course around what my map described as a 'wilderness plantation'. It may be they have a curious notion of wilderness around Cadder, because the plantation hid the local municipal dump and the road was busy with cars laden with old mattresses, washing machines and all sorts of domestic junk. After a couple of miles of dodging cars I was even beginning to think fondly of the old towpath.

I was glad to be able to cut off the road and join the Kelvin Walkway. This route follows the River Kelvin out of Glasgow to Milngavie, my goal for the end of this leg of the walk. The Kelvin Walkway was easy to follow and it made a change to be following a regular path instead of a canal bank. I didn't see any other walkers and the path, like a lot of the footpaths I'd encountered on my walk which are close to major centres of population, seemed a little unloved. There were broken fences, stiles in need of repair and evidence of some fly-tipping.

I reached Milngavie by late afternoon and thankfully sank onto one of the benches at the railway station, the end of the Borders leg of the walk. I caught the next train into Glasgow and walked up Sauchiehall Street amongst the

Saturday shoppers feeling grubby, travel-stained and quite out of place. My fleece was faded, my walking trousers were lacklustre, grubby and mud-stained, but none of this mattered. This battle scarred kit had been tried and tested from the cliffs of Cornwall through to the Pentland Hills. I looked a bit of a mess, but I was a happy mess. No wonder they asked me to pay upfront before they'd let me into the hotel.

The West Highland Way

If the start of the Pennine Way is something of an understated affair – simply touch base at the Old Nag's Head and set off walking in the direction of Kinder Scout – the start of the West Highland Way is an altogether much grander event.

In the middle of the pedestrian precinct at Milngavie three lads, one holding a Styrofoam cup of coffee, were having their photograph taken in front of a polished granite monolith. Two of them carried small day packs and all three were wearing trainers. As passers-by sat down to watch on one of the two commemorative benches we, that is the three lads and I, progressed, in some triumph, through a ceremonial arch, proudly emblazoned with the words 'West Highland Way', and descended a short ramp which deposited us, with rather less ceremony, in the bay at the back of the shops where a couple of white vans were unloading. From this point onwards the route became a little less clear. There was a likely-looking path leading off to the left or there was the roadway which the vans used for access. The lad with the coffee asked me which path I thought it was. As the map seemed unclear on this point I suggested we try the path on the left. It took us beside a pleasant gurgling stream, past another couple of benches, described a tight semicircular turn and deposited us back in the unloading bay some thirty seconds later.

'Was that it?' said the lad without the day pack. 'I'll have my certificate now?'

'Do we get a certificate?' said the lad with the Styrofoam coffee.

Once we were clear of the unloading bay it became apparent that there were a lot of walkers setting out on the West Highland Way that morning. The three lads stormed on ahead and I wouldn't see them again until the top end of Loch Lomond.

The route wound its way through Mugdock Wood, where there were still a few bluebells out, on past Craigallian and Carbeth Lochs and swerved around the dumpy tree-covered hill of Dumgoyach. It was a mild but damp sort of a day, what the Irish might call a 'soft' morning.

About seven miles out from Milngavie I observed some interesting behaviour amongst the groups of walkers on the track ahead of me. They would all stop by a signpost, study it carefully for a couple of minutes then, after what could only be described as a furtive look around, they would climb over a stile and head away from the main drag at some speed along a sidetrack off to the right and then they would disappear into a jumble of grey industrial-looking buildings two or three hundred yards away. I don't remember ever seeing any of them return. When I reached the sign I found it was for the Glengoyne Distillery, tempting walkers to stop 'for a dram to help you on your way'. Not being in any way lacking in the moral fibre department I naturally resisted the temptation and kept going. I kept going, that is, for all of half a mile, to the point where the main path passed the Beech Tree Inn and there my resolution weakened and I stopped and went in for a beer.

I would have liked to call it a day when I reached Drymen, which was at about the twelve mile mark. It seemed quite enough for the first day but I knew that the next day's walk was going to be a long haul all the way along the shores of Loch Lomond, so I pressed on to Balmaha beside the loch to try and give myself a bit of a head start.

If I could have found somewhere to stay halfway along Loch Lomond I would have done so, and I would have spread the walk over two days. But the youth hostel at Rowardennan was full and I'd drawn a blank at the Inversnaid Hotel so I had to tackle the whole twenty-one miles to Inverarnan in one go and by the time I got there I'd had more than enough of the 'Bonny, Bonny Banks'.

I had been warned about the path alongside Loch Lomond, especially the last bit at the far end, where the loch begins to narrow. Anna and Dirk had walked the West Highland Way a year earlier and said it was the worst path they'd ever been on, and a walker I was talking to outside the Oak Tree Inn at Balmaha told me in no uncertain terms that I needed my head examining if I was trying to walk it in one go. He offered me a lift in the taxi he and his wife were taking to Rowardennan. I gave him my most confident End to End walker's smile, picked up my rucksack and strode off trying to look heroic. It was only a path beside the lake after all. It couldn't be as bad as all that. It *was* as bad as all that; in fact it was worse. They were right, and I was wrong. The path along the side of Loch Lomond, and especially the bit beyond the Inversnaid Hotel, is as rough as any path I have ever come across. It was as bad as a path can possibly be, and still be able to call itself a path.

It started off innocently enough, a good broad track

alongside the loch with a few short, sharp climbs, but nothing to worry about. I made Rowardennan easily by lunchtime. Then there was a substantial path which climbed steadily through the conifer forest and then, having lulled me into a false sense of security, it became a narrow and steep scramble. There were huge boulders to climb over, under or around. There were teetering banks, sudden drops and all nicely greased with sludge. Hidden tree roots were something of a speciality, an inch or two off the ground, poking out from the mud and just at boot-tripping height. You couldn't afford to let your concentration lapse, not for even a minute. I've been on alpine scrambles, roped to a mountain guide, balancing on metal pitons and fixed wire hawsers which were less exacting than the Loch Lomond path.

It took me until four o'clock in the afternoon to reach the Inversnaid Hotel, where I instantly forgave them for not having a bed for me because the bar was open. I gulped down a pint of beer and a Kit Kat, the cornerstone of any End to End walker's diet, and quickly pressed on.

If anything the path gets worse from there for a couple of miles before it starts to flatten out and become more open woodland near the Inverarnan end of the loch and it was there, in a clearing by a stream, that I caught up with the three lads again, minus any cups of coffee this time. All three of them now had boots and huge backpacks, and I've no idea how their tiny day packs magically transformed into the sort of rucksacks which even Bryn from the Pennine Way might have considered excessive. They were not at that moment actually carrying the packs on their backs. The rucksacks had been discarded on the ground and two of the lads were flaked out next to them.

One of the guys on the deck hitched himself up onto an elbow as I passed and asked me how far it was to the

Drovers. Then he flopped back down on the ground again.

I took my map out and showed him where I thought we were and how far we had to go to the pub, the Drovers.

'But that's miles away.' There was a plaintive whine in his voice. I might have just told him he had to walk to the moon.

I pushed on and ten minutes later, one of the lads, the only one who was still standing, stormed past me muttering something about how his feet were killing him and the other two were pissing about. When I reached the campsite at Beinglas Farm he was sitting on his rucksack still muttering to himself and presumably waiting for his mates.

It was 8.10pm when I arrived at my B&B. I was scratched, I was sore, I was muddy and the back of my shirt had a huge white salt sweat stain where my rucksack had rested. I knocked on the door, but there was nobody at home. They had left me a note telling me where my room was so I went in, dumped my pack and, not stopping even to run a comb through my hair, went over the road to the pub, hoping they would still be serving food.

It may just have been the relief I was feeling after what had been a testing day, but I instantly fell in love with the Drovers. According to the tee shirts worn by the bar staff it had been 'Scottish Pub of the Year' in 1705. In terms of pubs of character, what the Tan Hill Inn is to the Pennine Way, the Drovers is to the West Highland Way. Inside the front door I was greeted by a rampant, snarling grizzly bear (thankfully long dead and stuffed) and there was a stuffed golden eagle perched on the end of the bar. All of the bar staff were, predictably, Aussies, and all were, also predictably, wearing kilts. The chap who served me was such a thoroughly stereotypical Australian, in the time it took him to pull me a pint of beer and take my food order, he managed to call me 'mate' six times.

There was a fire burning in the grate and candles flickering on each table filling the room with a soft smoky light. Over everything there was a patina of age. The Drovers is not rustic Olde Worlde Scotland for the tourists, it's the real thing. Rob Roy McGregor *really* did hang out there. The notched and battered claymores fixed to the walls looked as if they truly had seen service during the Jacobite Rebellion. The stuffed and mounted hunting trophies were animals which had been dead long before I was born and the oil paintings, usually of stern and serious-looking Scots men and women, had become faded and blackened with age. Above my seat there was a painting where you could only just make out the subject as a small dog, a terrier, not unlike Greyfriars Bobby, and next to that there was the skull and horns from a sable antelope with a plaque beneath which read, 'Blue Nile 1908, NAOE Scots Guards'.

An elderly gent in a tweed jacket stopped by my table and peered at the painting on the wall behind me.

'That painting,' he said to me, 'that painting of the dog.' He took off his glasses and leaned forward to look at it even closer. 'You know it's almost not there.'

A Clean Pan is a Happy Pan

Next morning the midges were bad. My notebook for that day was a testament to how bad they were. It makes for difficult reading, not because it is hard to read the writings of a man so obviously in the throws of torment, but because the page seems to have been peppered by commas, apostrophes and semi-colons in a scattergun fashion. On closer inspection they are not commas and semi-colons, they are the mortal remains of dozens of squashed mozzies.

The Scottish midge, especially in the months of May

and June, are the bane of the Highland walker. But in recent years there has been something of a revolution in the dark art of repelling this malevolent beastie. The old cattle drovers used to use bog myrtle, but if you've ever smelt bog myrtle you'd realise why nobody was ever very keen to sit next to a drover in the pub. Commercial insect repellents may be pretty good against the sub-Saharan malaria-carrying mosquito but not against the Scottish mozzie. In fact nothing worked very well, not, that is, until the discovery that Avon's Skin So Soft was so devilishly effective against midges. And it's not even supposed to be a mozzie cream. It's a lotion designed to be put on after a shower to moisturise the skin. Knowing that I was doing the Scottish part of the walk, my mum had kindly made me a present of a bottle of Skin So Soft before I set out so, sitting on a boulder in the sun, writing up my journal, just down the valley from Beinglas Farm, I tried it out for the first time. And the mozzies loved it.

I only had an easy stroll over the hill to Crianlarich, and even though the sun was shining I found my footsteps dragging. It wasn't just weariness after my exertions of the previous day alongside Loch Lomond, it was also a certain reluctance to get to my destination. The fact is, Crianlarich and I have history.

It was years ago, back in the 1970s, and my first trip on my own up to Scotland. It hadn't started well. A train had been cancelled, which caused a knock-on effect on the whole journey. I missed my connection and had to hitchhike to Carlisle. I made it to Glasgow but the train north broke down twice and by then I was so late that I knew I would never make it to Fort William before the youth hostel closed. When the train limped into Crianlarich I decided to get off there because some passengers had told me there was a youth hostel right next to the station.

Back in those days the warden of Crianlarich Youth Hostel was a disciplinarian and a fundamentalist in the pursuit of all the tenets espoused in the *Scottish Youth Hostels Association's Handbook*. He was a thin, dried-up man with crew cut hair and the bulging eyes of a fanatic. When the hostel opened its doors he would be there to meet each hosteller as they arrived and first of all their sheet sleeping bags had to pass a thorough inspection to ensure they met the regulation standard. If your sleeping bag failed on any count at all he made you hire one. And then when the hostellers were cooking he would stand over them and make sure everyone washed and scrubbed their pans until they were spotless *before* they were even allowed to sit down and eat. The food at Crianlarich was always as cold as the welcome. He was a stickler for cleanliness and had slogans pasted all over the walls urging youth hostellers to be cleaner, better and more wholesome people. I remember one with a cartoon of Snoopy looking at his face reflected in a shining frying pan with the caption: '*A Clean Pan is a Happy Pan*'.

One night of this would have been bad enough but the next day was Sunday and there were no trains running. To make matters worse I didn't have a map for the Crianlarich area so I wasn't even able to have much of a walk when the warden threw everyone out into the rain and locked the doors at ten o'clock sharp in the morning.

I was a bit early so I called in the tea room at the railway station then walked through the town, which in Crianlarich takes all of three minutes. A sense of déjà vu washed over me as the memories came flooding back. This time, I promised myself, it would be different, as I cast the youth hostel a sidelong glance and headed for a B&B instead.

It had taken me until this far in the walk to work out that whilst the owners of B&Bs are always ready to recommend somewhere for you to go and eat in the evening, sometimes these same owners of B&Bs have fallouts, rivalries and little vendettas with other local hoteliers and restaurateurs, and these local politics can influence where they recommend you go to eat. So I'd decided that the best policy was to listen very carefully to what they suggested and then do the exact opposite. According to the owner of the B&B there was a pub and two sizeable hotels in town which served food; the pub was good, one hotel was good and the other was okay, unless the chef was having a bit of an off day. I opted for the iffy one and was so glad I did, not because of the food, but because it proved to be the top spot in Crianlarich for people watching.

First of all there were the hotel staff. There seemed to be an awful lot of them, considering the amount of trade. At the bar was Svetlana, who was from somewhere in Eastern Europe. She was small and sharply pretty, with perfect make-up and a smile which never touched her eyes. Whatever drink I ordered she always replied, 'Of course.' Every time she set a drink down in front of me it was with the command, 'Enjoy.' But her helpfulness didn't extend as far as taking my order for a bar meal. There can be a strict hierarchy in some hotels which is incomprehensible to anyone outside the industry and she made it clear, without saying it in so many words, that food orders were not her job. They had waitresses for that sort of thing.

A second girl, also from Eastern Europe I thought, although as she was never allowed to speak I really couldn't tell, was short and had brightly hennaed hair. Her job seemed to consist of dashing into the bar every five minutes carrying a huge tray of clean glasses, swapping them for an equally big tray of dirty glasses and dashing out again. Then there were the two waitresses. The first was Emma, a tall, slim English girl with short dark hair, whose job was to shuttle between the bar and the dining room and share all the gossip with Svetlana. No matter how many times I tried smiling at her nothing would induce her to come over so I could order something to eat.

Pareto's Law states that in any working environment twenty percent of the staff do eighty percent of the work; that twenty percent was Fiona, the other waitress. I got the impression that she was a local girl, she spoke with a soft Scottish accent and was the only one wearing an apron. She walked into the bar drying her hands on a towel and Svetlana whispered something to her, something about me wanting to order a meal I think. She turned to me, smiled, said, 'Hello' and got out her pad straight away and took my order for a plate of haggis, neeps and tatties.

Across the bar from me sat a heavily-built man with a full beard and dressed in a grey business suit. He ordered a starter from Fiona and asked to see the wine list, then he took a mobile phone out of his jacket pocket and went outside to make a call. His starter and the wine list arrived but he was nowhere in sight. The girls seemed quite unsure of what to do. They went into a little huddle to discuss tactics.

I went up to the bar to order another drink.

'Of course,' said Svetlana.

Seeing they were in a bit of a quandary I told them that the bearded man was across the road in the car park, talking on his mobile. They went over to the window to take a look then went back into another huddle.

Svetlana placed a glass of white wine in front of me. I'd ordered red. 'Enjoy,' she said.

'Do I go tell him his food's here?' Fiona asked me. They had another meeting and decided that she should be dispatched to the hotel steps to shout him. He finished his call, came back to bar and started to eat his meal without acknowledging her. He didn't order any wine.

I had eaten my haggis, neeps and tatties, drunk my wine and was contemplating a pudding when the doors of the bar flew open and in bounded a group of four people, their faces all flushed from the outdoors. I took them to be a family. There was mother, who never spoke. She was late forties, short, with greying hair. Two teenage lads, awkward and gangly, dressed in tee shirts, jeans and trainers. And, clearly in charge of the whole group, a tall, striking woman of about thirty years old, with long blonde hair, who exuded energy and had the natural ability to fill any room she walked into. My guess was that she was the lads' elder sister.

'Do you remember us?' she said to Fiona. The words came out in a breathless rush.

'Err ... yes,' said Fiona, her face blank.

'We stayed here on the way up?'

'Err ... yes,' said Fiona again.

'Can you find us a table for dinner? We've just climbed Ben Nevis.'

Fiona said she'd see what she could do and rushed out. The blonde woman went over to the bar and ordered drinks for the whole family from Svetlana. Cokes for the boys, gin and tonic for mother and she had a white wine spritzer.

'Ben Nevis was sensational,' she said to everyone in the bar and to the world at large. 'Fantastic weather, bright sunshine, I wore my shorts all the way – look, I'm sunburnt.' She hitched up one trouser leg to reveal five inches of red, angry-looking calf. The drinks arrived.

'Enjoy,' said Svetlana.

The blonde woman knocked her spritzer straight back and ordered another.

'Of course,' said Svetlana.

'I've got some great photos.' She said and dug into a gold, Gucci handbag the size of a bucket and produced a tiny digital camera. 'Look, fantastic views over Loch Linnie, and over Loch Long.' She showed them first to Svetlana, and then to Emma and then went around the bar showing them to everyone. 'And then near the top we had to cross this snowfield. Michael,' she nodded in the direction of one of the teenage lads, 'slipped down on his arse.' Everyone was treated to a view of the snowfield and another of poor Michael on his arse. Michael glowered at her and buried his nose into his glass of coke. Then Fiona came in and announced she had found a table for them in the dining room so they picked up their drinks, bucket-sized handbag and digital camera and followed her out. When they had gone the bar seemed empty and all the customers who were left felt a little bit shellshocked. It was as if a tornado had just blown through.

As I went outside to make my way back to the B&B I saw the three Styrofoam lads tumble out of the pub and load first their rucksacks, then themselves, into a taxi and drive away. They didn't wave.

The 'Bradford' Group

I first noticed the 'Bradford' Group when I was having breakfast at the Bridge of Orchy Hotel. It was the painful way in which Toby walked across the room that drew my attention to him. He walked in a jerky fashion, knees and elbows jabbing upwards, like a man walking barefoot over hot coals. He was tall, thin and had something of a scholarly air about him. His black, tightfitting tracksuit only seemed to emphasise his thinness. He joined four other people at the table next but one to me. As he sat down there were sympathetic murmurings and looks of concern from Chrissie and Tina, two of the three women sitting there. At the head of the table, concentrating on the food on his plate and taking no part in the conversation, was a beetle-browed, thickset man. He had the air of a man in charge; breakfast, for him, seemed more akin to chairing a meeting. I never discovered his name; the others I learnt a little about over the next few days. His wife, Lynne, sitting next to him and also not joining in the other women's concern for Toby, was in her early forties, blonde-haired, and wearing the latest in technical fleeces. Chrissie, who, with Tina, was fussing over Toby, was from Aberdeen originally, in her late thirties and wore her hair pulled back into a ponytail. She had a slightly haggard face which looked as if it may have been quite pretty once, and could be again if she gave up on her habit of always scowling. And finally there was Tina, a short, rotund woman from Portugal with her dark hair drawn into a tight bun at the nape of her neck. She was doing the walk to lose some weight and, like Toby, was finding it a painful experience.

After breakfast they set off walking just ahead of me, all carrying day packs. They crossed the Bridge of Orchy itself and took the path up into the forest. I expected that I would soon overtake them, not because I was walking particularly fast, but because a walker on his own always tends to cover the ground quicker than a group, but in this instance I didn't. I climbed up through the trees, spotting a couple of deer along the way, and walked onto the summit of Mam Carraigh, where I stopped to take in the view over Loch Tulla. It was a clear day, fantastic for views, warm but with a high layer of cloud which was stopping the sun from breaking through. I dropped down onto a good path to Victoria Bridge and still saw nothing of the group; I assumed they had gone another way.

To me Rannoch Moor has always represented everything which is wild and untamed about Scotland. Many years ago I'd been over this way on the bus from Glasgow to Glen Coe but I'd never crossed it on foot. I was excited and just a little apprehensive. The owner of the B&B in Crianlarich had told me that it was a good track all the way.

'A good route,' he had said, 'but featureless, nothing much in the way of landmarks. You cross one bridge halfway along and that's about it.'

It took me three hours of steady walking to cross Rannoch Moor and he was right, there were no landmarks except Ba Bridge, and I could easily have missed that if I hadn't been looking out for it. Also there was no shelter and I didn't like to think what the crossing could be like on a wet and windy day. The moor was a wild and open expanse of heather and bog, with high hills fringing the horizon and seeming to encircle it.

I finally topped the rise near Gualaan Liath Ghiubhais and could see Glen Coe and Kinghouse in the distance. It was tempting to press straight on to the pub but first I wanted to take my own photo of what must be Scotland's most famous image, a shot of Buachaille Etive Mor with Blackrock Cottage in the foreground. Versions of this photograph crop up on calendars, in guidebooks (there was one in my West Highland Way guidebook) and on the lids of biscuit tins the world over. As an image which epitomises the Highlands, it is hard to beat. Buachaille Etive Mor (I believe this is Gaelic for the Shepherd of Glen Coe) is a graceful cone of rock and scree sweeping up to a sharp peak. But it is no fragile alp, it's a beefy no nonsense hill. You don't muck about with Buachaille Etive Mor, not if you know what's good for you. It sits amongst the heather and boulders where Rannoch Moor and Glen Coe meet, with Blackrock Cottage, which must be everyone's picture of the perfect whitewashed Highland cottage, as a focal point in front. I fired off a dozen photos, none of them being the perfect shot I was hoping for because there were two cars parked outside the cottage and I had to manoeuvre to try and find a position where I could keep them out of shot. Photography over, I headed for Kingshouse and the Climbers' Bar.

This was another long day's walk, which again I would have split over two days if I could have stayed at Kingshouse, the only accommodation for the tent-less for miles around. But Kingshouse was full because (and this was beginning to become a bit of a tedious pattern by now), I had arrived on the weekend of the Caledonian Challenge. Just for the record, the Caledonian Challenge is a twenty-four hour, fifty-four-mile walk or run from Gairlochy (on the Caledonian Canal beyond Fort William) to Auchtertyre (which I'd passed through the previous day, not long after Crianlarich).

When I walked into the Climbers' Bar the 'Bradford' group were already on their second pint and halfway through their plates of pie and chips. The chairman and his wife were talking to a bearded chap wearing a red tee shirt, who, even I could tell, was walking End to End. The big giveaway was that he had 'End to End 2' printed across his tee shirt and two flags, a Union Jack and the Saltire, fixed to the top of his rucksack. I ordered myself a drink and sat on another table, periodically catching snatches of their conversation.

Not to be outdone by the End to End walker the

chairman was telling him what good time they were making, how they were aiming to do the West Highland Way in four and a half days (it took me six days). It seemed the chairman and his wife were the experienced walkers, and Toby, Tina and Chrissie were not. The chairman was holding forth while the End to Ender kept his own council; Toby, Tina and Chrissie didn't look up from their chips. I left the pub before them all, mindful that I still had a long way to go.

The track ran parallel to the road through Glen Coe for a couple of miles to Altnafeadh. Less than a mile out from Kinghouse the 'Bradford' group overtook me, all going like the clappers, and not long after that the first of the Caledonian Challenge runners started to pass me going in the opposite direction. From Altnafeadh the route takes to the hills again, climbing the Devil's Staircase. It always amuses me how we attach melodramatic labels to perfectly natural and quite un-satanic features. I blame the Victorian's love of all things Gothic myself. Anywhere can be made just that bit more dramatic by attaching words like 'Hell' or 'Devil' to it. Back in Cornwall I'd stopped at Hell's Mouth, that was just a café by a gap in the cliffs. Not far from Crowden and just off the Pennine Way I'd been around the Devil's Elbow (twice actually), which was, well, just a bend in the road. And here, on the West Highland Way, we had the Devil's Staircase.

'We've got to go over the Devil's Staircase next,' said one of the Caledonian Challengers in a quavering voice. She was labouring up the hill from Kinlochleven.

'I know,' said her mate. She looked on the point of bursting into tears. 'And I'm just dreading it,'

'Relax,' said Gaz, 'it's only a zigzag path down the hillside, that's all.'

By this time I'd hooked up with Gaz, the End to End

walker I'd met in the Climber's Bar at Kinghouse. He had overtaken me walking up the Devil's Staircase then, ten minutes later, I found him at the top, leaning back against the cairn with his boots off, taking a break and generally soaking up the view back down Glen Coe.

He was a retired soldier and this was his second End to End raising money for the Army Benevolent Fund. He had plans to walk End to End every year for ten years. After reading Tony Hawke's book, *Around Ireland with a Fridge*, he was thinking of walking it with a tumble dryer next time.

We walked into Kinlochleven together and Gaz's walk received quite a bit of attention from the Caledonian Challengers we met during the afternoon, many of whom were squaddies. They would stop, do a double take, look at the flags flying from his pack and at the logo on his tee shirt and say something like, 'You're walking Land's End to John O'Groats?'

'Yep,' said Gaz, 'I'm raising money for the Army Benevolent Fund.'

'Great,' said the Caledonian Challengers.

'We're both walking End to End in fact.' And they would notice me for the first time. 'I'm trying to walk it in sixty days,' said Gaz.

Which was my cue to say, 'And I'm trying to walk it in three years.'

Next morning, in the breakfast room at MacDonald's Hotel in Kinlochleven Tina and Chrissie were sitting at the table next to me. Chrissie stared into space, moodily stirring her coffee. Tina toyed with a piece of toast but didn't seem to have much appetite. There was no sign of the other three from the 'Bradford' group. Tina and Chrissie seemed to have struck up a friendship with some kayakers on the next table. One of them walked over and gave Tina a hug and asked how she was feeling.

'Depressed,' she said, 'depressed and sore.'

'We're going to ride over to Fort William after breakfast with the luggage bus,' said Chrissie. 'Tina's knees went yesterday afternoon and now my legs have gone.'

'It's not like we're experienced walkers,' said Tina. 'We left Milngavie four days ago and we've been doing more than twenty miles a day.'

'Fifteen miles a day would have been all right,' said Chrissie, 'we could have managed that.'

'The others set out at six o'clock this morning to walk to Fort William,' said Tina. 'Then we are all catching the twelve-thirty train back home.'

'I think,' said Chrissie, 'I'll see if I can sell my boots on eBay.'

Fort William and the Ben

I woke to the sound of rain pattering against my window. It was a misty, moist and very midgy, morning. The air was very still, with a light drizzle and long fingers of mist which clung to the surface of the loch. I didn't have any mozzie repellent because, in an effort to save weight, I'd ditched the bottle of Skin So Soft my mum had bought me at the Bridge of Orchy. The manageress of the hotel at Kinlochleven told me it was an especially bad year for midges. She also told me where I'd been going wrong with my Skin So Soft.

'You have to absolutely slather yourself in the stuff,' she said, 'and it doesn't work by repelling the midges. It works by making your skin so slippery and greasy the little blighters can't get enough of a foothold to be able to bite you.'

I bought some Tropical Formula from the hotel shop instead. That didn't work either.

I tried rolling my shirt sleeves down, rolling my socks up and rolling my trouser legs down. I pulled my hat down over my eyes and any exposed inch of skin I doused in Tropical Formula, but still nothing would keep the ravenous little beasties off. It wasn't too bad when I was moving but when I stopped to take a photo or put my cagoule on or take it off, and this was an activity I was engaged in a lot because it was another of those on and off rainy days, the flying hordes would descend and eat me alive.

I was making a slow start, what with the previous day's long walk over Rannoch Moor and climbing the, not so devilish, Devil's Staircase. As I laboured up the hill through the trees and out of Kinlochleven, swatting midges as I went, I thought about Gaz and how a professional End to Ender like him would no doubt have stormed miles ahead. Ten minutes later when I had stopped again to either take my cag off or put it back on, I saw his orange cagoule coming over the crest of the hill behind me. It seemed everyone was a bit slow off the mark that morning.

We walked on together as the track wound around the lower slopes of Stob Ban through quite open trees at first, then later denser forest until the path started the descent into Glen Nevis. At one point we stopped and looked across the valley, where we could see Ben Nevis and the hoards of walkers, who from that distance looked like ants, making their way up the tourist route.

'You know I might just join them tomorrow,' I said to Gaz. 'It would be nice to climb the big one.'

A mile or so later Gaz cut off to the right down the path which led to the head of the glen and the campsite, and I pressed on down the valley. The walk down Glen Nevis seemed endless especially the last bit along the road, but just beyond the distillery on the outskirts of Fort William, and at 4.05pm, I reached the sign which marked the end of the West Highland Way.

Climbing Ben Nevis does not generally form part of most End to Ends, but it would, or so I rationalised, clear up the tricky matter of what would be the highest point of the walk above sea level (which, as weak excuses go, must be one of the weakest), plus it seemed a shame to walk all the way through Scotland and not climb at least one Munro. It's easy to be sniffy about climbing the Ben just because so many people do it each year and, of course, most of them do just climb it because it is the highest. I'd only been up the Ben once before and that was on my first trip to Scotland with George White, who was a friend from my rambling club days in Sheffield. George knew his way around Scotland so we used his tent, camped in Glen Nevis, did the Ben on just our second day in Scotland and then pushed on along the Road to the Isles, along Loch Arkaig and Loch Morar and then over to the Isle of Skye, where we were washed out by the rain. So a trip up the highest hill in the UK would be something of a reminder of my first expedition to the far north.

Next morning I retraced my steps back towards the end of the West Highland Way and almost immediately bumped into Gaz walking in the other direction. We shook hands and wished each other well. He would be in John O'Groats a long time before me; his End to End finally took him sixty-two days.

I headed first for the visitor centre and then I became one of the long column of walkers making their way up the tourist route towards the summit. At the visitor centre they said to allow four hours up and three hours down. It took me three hours, forty minutes up and three and a half hours down. It was the ideal day for a big hill: warm, sunny and just enough breeze to keep the midges at bay. Ben Nevis is 1,344 metres high or 4,406 feet, if you prefer it in old money. The tourist route is a good, broad stony track which works its way up the glen, around the front of the lochan and then up the main buttresses of the mountain. What is most noticeable is just how far up it is. You crest one rise and look ahead and there is always a bit more hill, usually a lot more hill, up there in front of you. The Ben is so high that there is always some snow on the top, even in high summer, and a short way before the summit I found, and crossed, the snowfield which had so delighted the blonde-haired woman who had breezed into the hotel in Crianlarich four days earlier. A band of snow and ice, about a hundred metres across, covered a steep slope fifty metres below the summit. A set of slushy footsteps cut diagonally across so I set off kicking steps into the ice and with my trekking pole in hand and my sunglasses perched on my nose I felt very alpine.

Shortly beyond the snowfield I reached the summit cairn and for a few minutes I was the highest person in Britain. Then I took the camera out and after I had taken digital photos of Loch Linnie and Loch Long, and descended back down the tourist route, I too breezed into the bar (in my case the bar of the Ben Nevis Inn) just as flushed, just as windblown and every bit as elated as my blonde-haired friend had been.

After a beer I followed the single track road back to Fort William. Where it runs into a housing estate at Claggan, parked in a side street was a minibus belonging to the Lochaber Phoenix Boxing Club. Painted on the side was their motto, which I believe was first coined by Vince Lombardi, and one which applies just as much to the End to Ender: 'Winners never quit, quitters never win'.

Across the Great Divide

If you like fir trees, I mean if you *really, really* like fir trees; if the very thought of the mighty spruce, the Douglas fir, the Scots pine and Christmas trees of every conceivable size, shape and description just sets your pulses a-racing; if your idea of heaven is mile after mile of dark brooding tree trunks crowding in from every side; if you like nothing better than dense mats of pine needles blotting out the light and tree trunks blocking your view of the hills, the loch and anything else for that matter ... then ... it might be that the Great Glen Way is just the walk for you.

The route of the Great Glen Way follows the natural fault line which splits Scotland diagonally in two from Fort William to Inverness. It also ran right past my bedroom window in Fort William so starting out was a simple matter of picking up my rucksack, crossing the car park, climbing over the wire fence where it was squashed down a bit and heading for the banks of the Caledonian Canal.

Unlike most long distance trails I'd done so far the Great Glen Way does not get on with the job. It faffs around for ages, wandering all around the backstreets of Fort William, along the banks of the River Lochy, over Soldier's Bridge and past the ruins of Inverlochy Castle before it finally reaches the canal. I'd become bored long before then so I missed out one of the official route's time-wasting loops, took a shortcut and scrambled up a steep bank to join the towpath just before Banavie and the eight locks which make up Neptune's Staircase.

The walk alongside the Caledonian Canal and past Neptune's Staircase is another walk I did with George on my first trip to Scotland. It was back in the days when I was still quite new to photography so when I spotted a substantial ship working its way through the locks it seemed to me a pretty good subject for a photo. The skipper came out onto the wing of the bridge and shouted down to me, 'Get some good photos?'

'Yes,' I said, 'hope so.'

'Send me one of the boat?'

'Okay.'

The skipper went back into the wheelhouse, wrote his address on a scrap of paper, put it in an empty cigarette packet and threw it down to me on the towpath. When the film was processed there were three photos of the ship, none of them very good but at least you could see what they were meant to be. Anybody trying to be serious about photography in those days always took slides, and I remember it was quite expensive to have the photos of the boat made from slides into prints. I was an apprentice working for Sheffield Corporation Parks and Gardens Department back then so I didn't earn very much. I posted them off but I never heard back from the skipper. As I made my way along the Caledonian Canal I couldn't help thinking about this and wondering whether he ever received them. I remember his address was Port Erin on the Isle of Man.

It was pleasant and level walking alongside the canal under the mature, broad-leaved trees which fringed the path. On the far bank, and on the hillside opposite, like highlights amongst the green were scattered patches of bright yellow gorse bushes in full bloom.

The Moy Swing Bridge was something of an antique and still powered by hand. I stopped to talk to the bridge keeper, a stocky, bearded man wearing a blue seafaring jumper. He was sitting on a bench outside enjoying the sun and eating a salad with a fork from out of a Tupperware box. I'd noticed that a dozen or so walkers, well kitted out and sporting big packs, had passed me going in the opposite direction, so I asked him how popular the Great Glen Way was.

'Oh it's really popular,' he said. 'In the summer walkers come past me here every four or five minutes. Aye, you'll be in for a good day tomorrow, walking alongside the loch, if the weather holds.'

The weather did hold and there were bits of Loch Lochy to see, just occasionally through the trees, but from Clunes to Laggan seven miles away, the track was walled in by conifers on either side with scarcely a landmark to give any indication of progress for mile after energy-sapping mile. When I emerged from the trees at the far end of Loch Lochy, blinking and disorientated, I came across a noticeboard announcing that the Invergarry Link, along the north side of Loch Oich, was closed. I found out later that it was because they were cutting down a few of the trees so perhaps I should have been grateful. The noticeboard also stated that you must make alternative arrangements 'at your own expense.' This was not good news because I'd booked to stay at Invergarry and, the next day, I was planning to follow the Invergarry Link, along the north side of Loch Oich. So the logging would mean I'd need to backtrack around the head of Loch Oich and then walk all the way along the south shore of the loch, a five mile detour, so you wouldn't find me marching along cheerfully singing the 'Lumberjack Song'.

At first glance the only thing that marked the Well of the Seven Heads out from any other old monument was that it had a shop named after it. Yet in Scotland, where they do rather specialise in history of the more gruesome variety, it would win the prize for the most grizzly monument. It appeared that one way to wheedle your way in favour with the clan chieftain, back in the old days, was to round up seven murderers, decapitate them, and then, because nobody likes to receive a grubby severed head, give them all a wash where the stream runs into Loch Oich, before you make the clan chief a present of them. It's quite enough to put you off your dinner, I thought, as I bought a vanilla Magnum from the Well of the Seven Heads shop and munched it as I walked along the road to Invergarry.

At the far end of Loch Oich I swapped the trees for a long open section of the Caledonian Canal where some enterprising person had pinned up handwritten signs on the trees beside the canal: 'Bottles of Avon Skin So Soft, at supermarket prices, on sale at the cottage'.

Fort Augustus marked the start of Loch Ness but as the path was straight back into the trees I really didn't see a great deal of it. I came up for air briefly at Invermoriston (last shop for thirty-five miles), where I stayed overnight before delving straight back into the pine woods and climbing steadily all through the morning until the path burst through the forest into the open heath and farmland above. I felt like taking in a deep breath, stretching and filling my lungs. Then, because you're never very far from a tree on the Great Glen Way, the path dropped back down through the trees again to Drumnadrochit.

You couldn't visit Drumnadrochit and not be aware of the legend of the Loch Ness Monster. For one thing there are two visitor centres which seem to be competing with one another, the Loch Ness Centre and the Loch Ness *Monster* Centre. I forget which one of the two claimed to be the original one.

The first sighting of Nessie was by St Columba in 565 AD and since then there have been thousands of newspaper column inches devoted to debates about whether or not Nessie exists, exclusive eyewitness accounts, dubious sightings and grainy indistinct photos which frankly could be of anything. I'm a born sceptic, but, next morning, as I climbed the hill out of Drumnadrochit, I spotted (and took a grainy indistinct photo of) a long line on the water not unlike the bow wave from a boat, except there was no boat out there, nor was there anything I could see which could have made such a bow wave. Personally I think it was a long slick of Avon Skin So Soft floating on the surface of the loch.

The Road to Hell

Suddenly I was on the last leg of the walk. Tired of long train journeys back and forth I decided to treat myself to a flight up to Inverness. I got a taxi from the airport back to my starting point by the statue of Flora MacDonald outside Inverness Castle. The taxi driver, noting my boots, rucksack and cagoule, asked me where I was heading. When I told her John O'Groats she was singularly unimpressed. 'John O'Groats?' she said. 'Ach, but there's nothing up there, just a stick and a hotel.'

The Kessock Suspension Bridge vibrated gently under my feet when the traffic rumbled past but there was a good cycle path to walk along so the traffic wasn't a problem. I stopped in the middle to take in the view back towards Inverness and watch a small fishing boat chugging out toward the sea, making slow progress as it pushed against the wind and tide.

On the far side of the bridge I came out onto the Black Isle, which isn't an island at all, it's a peninsula, and I spent the morning walking along beside the waters of the Beauly Firth. This turned out to be the best walking of the day.

The sunlight had a late summer golden quality to it. There was the smell of ozone in the air and a couple of blokes with fishing rods were sitting quietly beside the water. Herring gulls the size of turkeys were strutting along the shingle, occasionally a quarrel would break out amongst them and they would explode noisily into the air before settling back to earth again and carrying on their search for anything edible along the shoreline. As I looked back towards Kessock Bridge a veil of wispy vapour was drifting past, at a height of perhaps fifty feet, clear of the water but hiding the roadway and leaving the suspension towers sticking out like spindly legs above.

I followed a quiet road with almost no traffic along the water's edge and as the morning progressed I began to think about lunch. I must have passed a dozen or more excellent lunch spots further back but as I got towards the far end of the firth the road became sandwiched between a stone wall and the boggy shoreline so there was nowhere suitable to sit. A group of a dozen Canada geese flew up suddenly from amongst the reeds, wheeled around overhead and mocked me. They circled for a minute, flew out over the water then landed, each trailing a long silver wake behind. Through the remains of a hedge, on its side amongst the reeds, was a rusted oil drum and the only thing around which might remotely provide a seat for lunch. Water seeped up through the reeds but there was sufficient substance in the ground so that I was able to walk out to the oil drum without getting a wet foot. The top and bottom of the oil drum had rusted away but I could sit comfortably on the side and look out across the firth. The corroded metal had retained some elasticity and sitting on it felt a bit like bouncing along on an old sprung cart. Out in the still waters a grey seal popped its head up and looked longingly at my fishpaste sandwiches. I finished my lunch, waved goodbye to the seal and turned inland to pick my way through a jumble of back roads towards Conon Bridge and Dingwall. Then the weather turned nasty and the rain set in for the afternoon.

I made an unnecessary circuit of Dingwall, past the shops, the church and the level crossing, trying to square up the cycle route marked on my map and the cycle route, or the lack of it, on the ground, but this was no hardship, I'd rather taken to Dingwall. As I worked my way north I found I'd had to revise my views on Scottish towns. I'd always thought them to be, grey, solid, dreary-looking places, drab towns set amongst astounding hills and wonderful scenery, practical places yet deeply unattractive. But after passing through towns like Melrose, Peebles and now Dingwall I was starting to see them in a different light. Charming, friendly and full of character, these were the sort of places where I would have liked to spend a bit more time. They were added to my ever growing list of places to come back to and visit again.

The Cromarty Firth gave an indication of the oil and gas industry offshore. It was a sort of aquatic parking lot for oil rigs. There were two of them moored out there with what looked like small boats and tenders buzzing around them. I had good views through the trees and out over the firth as I followed the B817, which ran along a wooded hillside above, and parallel to, the A826. I knew that this final leg of the walk would be almost entirely roadwalking. The options narrow the closer you get to the far northeast corner of Britain.

There were some big houses in this part of Scotland, usually somewhere high up on the hillside and half hidden by trees. Grand houses built of stone, houses with turrets, extensions, outbuildings and grand winding drives which terminated at the roadside in a pair of substantial carved stone gateposts. The kind of houses which couldn't quite make up their minds if they wanted to be a castle or a farmstead, and houses which were a testament to the aspiration, status and ambition of the people who built them. And there were clearly some where the aspiration, status and ambition had been misplaced. Where the houses were gone, the family had gone and the trees and the woodland had returned to reclaim the land. All that remained to give any clue of those lost hopes and ambitions were a set of solid stone gateposts, overgrown with moss and ivy, opening onto a tangled jungle of a once proud driveway which now led nowhere.

If you ignore the time I was very nearly squished by a coal wagon on the A389 outside Padstow, I'd managed to more or less avoid A roads up to this point of the walk, but by the time I reached Tain, I knew there would be no escape from them; and not just any old A road, but the bane of every End to Ender, the dreaded A9. Chris Rhea once wrote a song about the M25 called 'The Road to Hell'. I don't know if he ever came up to this corner of Scotland but I'm sure if he did he would instantly re-dedicate his song to the A9.

It started off by lulling me into a false sense of security. I joined it just beyond the town and there was something of a carnival atmosphere about the place as I walked along amongst the crowds who were making their way to the Glenmorangie and Tain Highland Gathering. This was a proper Highland gathering with bagpipes and marquees, and Highland dancing and caber tossing competitions. There were lots of people dressed in kilts, people who looked as if they wore kilts on an everyday basis, not just 'donning the old Highland regalia' for the benefit of the tourists. It would have been nice to stay and join in but really, I couldn't. I couldn't bottle out on the A9, not this soon.

A mile further on and there was yet another inducement to tempt the End to Ender away from the A9, a site which, to the whisky drinker, is frankly hallowed ground: the

Glenmorangie Distillery. I pressed on, promising myself a wee dram of the old Glenmorangie when I reached Dornoch. So a mile or two out, just when I was beginning to think this A9 lark wasn't so bad after all, it sent down a juggernaut so fast and so close its backdraught sent me staggering sideways off the hard shoulder and into the ditch. It quickly followed this up with a salvo of four HGVs, three white vans and a tractor. Then it threw down a squall of rain so sudden and so vicious it had soaked me while I was still hopping around on one leg trying to get the other leg into my waterproof overtrousers.

This became the pattern for the afternoon. Heavy, squally showers, and me head down slogging into the wind and the rain and dodging articulated wagons which were throwing up spray by the bucket load.

The bridge over the Dornoch Firth was nothing like as imposing as the Kessock Suspension Bridge. It was built on concrete piles low over the water. It was also very long, at least a mile, and offered no protection from the elements. Halfway along I passed the second of only two other End to End walkers I met on this final section of the walk. Well, I assumed he was an End to Ender, the only walkers you meet up there are End to Enders. He was a youngish chap, heading south and in the opposite direction to me, head down and looking very glum. He had long, straight hair and was dressed in drab ex-army type gear, with massive boots and a khaki waterproof cover over his pack.

Incidentally I think that I've spotted a subject here which is ripe for some serious research: End to End walkers and their waterproof rucksack covers. Every rucksack (apart from one or two specialist packs which are more like waterproof kit bags with shoulder straps attached) has one big serious design flaw, they all let the wet in. So walkers feel obliged to use a rucksack cover in wet weather. But End to End walkers keep them fixed to their packs *all* of the time, even when it's not raining. Pauline-Walking-for-Jesus, who I met a mile or so short of Alness, did. Gaz did. Gaz even kept his sandwiches tucked up inside his pack cover. And now this chap, the gloomiest End to Ender I'd ever met, had his pack cover firmly strapped in place. Personally, I loathe the damn things. I hate them nearly as much as waterproof overtrousers, and that's saying something. But, that afternoon, I have to admit, as I trudged over Dornoch Bridge my pack cover was also firmly tied onto my rucksack (with its trusty and indispensable bungy cord). And, much as I hate to admit it, the further I went on the walk, the more I found I was using my pack cover and not just when it was raining.

It seemed unthinkable that an End to Ender wouldn't stop for a chat, but the chap in the ex-army gear I met on Dornoch Bridge didn't. He had his iPod plugged into his ears, shoulders hunched, head down and gave me just a half-wave as we passed. I found myself thinking, is that what it does to you, is that what I'll be like soon, after a few more days of walking the A9?

The only bright spot of the afternoon was that just before the Dornoch Bridge I saw my first road sign for John O'Groats (eighty-five miles). I performed a little impromptu jig on the hard shoulder of the A9. A sight so unusual it caused a Dormobile to swerve and narrowly miss a bread van. Suddenly the whole thing looked as if it might just be possible.

Cry Wolf

I stayed at a pub in Dornoch where they gave me a huge room with a double bed, a single bed and, in a little offshoot room, yet another single bed. If I'd been staying there any longer I might have considered subletting.

A quiet back road took me out of town and along the southern edge of Loch Fleet, which is a long inlet of mudflats with strutting wading birds like oyster catchers and dunlin and, a short way offshore, portly seals hauled out on a sandbank. It was another of those times I wished I'd packed a pair of binoculars. A little further along I watched a weasel with russet fur and a white tip to its tail trot across the road a few yards ahead of me, quite oblivious to my presence, and then, like an Olympic high jumper, leap over the tall grass at the verge and disappear into the undergrowth beyond.

Much as I'd enjoyed my morning's nature ramble I knew it was only a temporary respite; I was soon back on my proper job, footslogging along the A9. Shortly after I regained the main road I crossed the Mound. This was a kind of raised embankment which sliced across the tail end of Loch Fleet and provided the traffic with a straight bit of road where they could really put their foot down.

By the time I'd reached Golspie I'd honed my A9 walking technique down to something of a fine art. I'd discovered the traffic tended to come in waves, or pods as I liked to think of them. Six or eight vehicles would all be bunched together, often they were being held up behind a car towing a caravan or a slow-moving, diesel-belching wagon. Then there would be a break when the road would be clear for three or four minutes perhaps and there would be no traffic at all. So whenever I saw a 'pod' of traffic approaching I'd stop walking and get as far onto the verge and away from the traffic as I could. I'd hang on tight to my hat, and any other loose or dangling bits of equipment, and wait while the wave of traffic sped past. Then, when the coast was clear, I'd emerge onto the edge of the tarmac and, walking facing the direction of the oncoming traffic, cover as much ground as I could until the next wave of traffic came trucking on down. The scariest time was when cars coming from behind overtook. I couldn't see them so couldn't avoid them and I had no idea when it was going to happen. And they would come unnervingly close. So close I could have easily reached out and touched them. So close that I could feel their slipstream tugging at my clothes.

Some cars were very considerate and would slow down or pull out and give me plenty of room. I tried to remember to wave to them. Others seemed oblivious to walkers. They would pass close to the curb and at speed. My worst A9 moment came shortly before Dunrobin Castle. I saw a pod of traffic approaching and watched as a car pulled out ahead to overtake a wagon. They were approaching rapidly, neither seemed to want to give way and the car was giving the wagon no room to pull out for me. There was not much verge at this point for me to take refuge in, just a few inches of rough ground from the kerb to a dry stone wall with a broken wire fence on top of it. I tried to get as far over into the wall as I could but for some reason my left leg had decided it wasn't going to follow me. The lorry, with the car abreast, was blocking the road completely now and bearing down on me fast, too fast. Shades of Brands Hatch come to Sutherland. I glanced into the cab of the lorry. The driver had a 'rabbit in the headlights' expression fixed on his face. He clearly hadn't seen me and he stared forwards in a glassy-eyed, unblinking fashion. I looked back to where my left leg was stretched out behind me. A length of rusty fence wire had wrapped itself around my leg and snagged on my trousers. I was caught and held fast like a deer in a poacher's snare. I could feel the sweat breaking out on my forehead; this was how disasters happen. My hands shook as I tried to untangle the wire. But it was held fast. No time for niceties, I heaved at my leg and with the sound of ripping cotton it suddenly came free. When I looked up the radiator grill of the wagon almost filled my vision, blotting out the sun. My leg free now, I lurched for the top of the stone wall, made it and lay there, eyes closed and clutching hold of one of the fence posts and the wire which had very nearly been my undoing. The wagon and car rushed past, still in line abreast, covering me with the dust, muck and dry leaves being swept along in their wake.

Then the traffic cleared and the A9 became quiet once more and the road took on the appearance of a riverbed in a drought. I climbed off the wall, dusted myself down, briefly inspected the rent in my trousers and, with legs shaking like two jellies in a trifle, I carried on walking north.

Before I set off on the day's walk I took a wander around Brora. I followed the village trail through the cottages, down to the sea and along to the harbour. It was more of an inlet really than a harbour, with an old boat tied up to the quay and nets, bits of old rope and lobster pots lying around. I was deliberately killing time because I knew I had a shorter walk, about eleven miles to Helmsdale, and I expected to cover the ground quite quickly. It's a factor of walking End to End, or any long trek for that matter: as the walk progresses you become more comfortable covering longer and longer distances. In the early days, back on the Cornish coast, I'd have been more than happy with eleven miles, but up there in Sutherland, it felt like just a half-day stroll. The length of the day's walk was dictated, as they had been for the entire walk, by the distance between places where I could find somewhere to stay, but now, as I was nearing the end, I had a feeling of wanting to 'go for it'. A short walk was a frustration, leaving me kicking my heels.

The final delight Brora had to offer was that I could leave town via a footpath between the golf course and the sea and have a mile or so of traffic-free walking before I had to rejoin that road which all End to Enders love to hate.

If I had to choose somebody from the past I would like to meet it would have to be the Duke of Portland KC, from the year 1924. I think he and I would have had a lot in common. I don't know if he had been made redundant (can a duke be made redundant?) or if he had taken early retirement, but like me he clearly had some time on his hands and was casting around for some constructive outlet to usefully fill that time. The Duke of Portland KC chose to erect commemorative stones around the county. He raised a stone marking Grey Hen's Well a little further along the A9, but his magnum opus was to be found in a lay-by a short way before Lothbeg. A modest, rough-hewn stone marked the spot where, on or around 1900, the last wolf in Sutherland may or may not have been killed. This memorial has a small but select band of aficionados (of which I am now happy to be one) and it earns a mention in nearly every End to End account. The stone cites a book, Scrope's *Art of Deerstalking*, and is a bit vague on details. Nobody seems quite sure where the wolf was killed, or when, or even if it was killed at all. But if the poor creature was done to death then, according to the memorial stone, the chap in the frame for the killing was a shady-sounding cove who went by the name of Hunter Polson.

The sea views and the wolf memorial brightened the

section of the road from Brora to Helmsdale. Some of the cars were also cheerfully honking their horns and waving at me as they passed, in no doubt where I was heading.

I stayed at a hotel in Helmsdale which was everything you would imagine a Highland hotel to be. Oak panelled walls, leather buttoned seats, hunting prints and dozens and dozens of antlers and stuffed mounted hunting trophies hanging on the walls. Even my room key was fixed to a pointy bit of stag's antler. Later that evening, when I was making my way back to my room after dinner, I discovered a drawing room on the first floor which was like something from an earlier, and much grander era. I could have imagined an Edwardian hunting party, in their plus fours and tweeds, relaxing in there. It was full of elegant antique furniture, brocaded couches and chaise longues. Above the fireplace was a massive stuffed elk's head with wide spreading antlers which must have been at least six feet across. The walls were positively groaning with mounted stag's heads all staring at me with that curious reproachful expression which stuffed animals always seem to have. It was like a temple to the taxidermists' art. I counted twenty-one stuffed stag's heads altogether. Next morning, after breakfast I couldn't resist another peep at the Edwardian drawing room, but in the cold light of day, I could only count nineteen stuffed stag's heads. Had someone crept in during the night and made off with an eight-pointer specimen tucked under each arm or had I just dreamt it, I was still in Glenmorangie country after all.

The Ord of Caithness

The day began with a steep climb out of Helsmdale and over a high sweeping stretch of coastline known as the Ord of Caithness. This is a land of legends. Fortunately the ghostly coaches of ill omen rattling over the Ord stayed away so the worst I had to contend with was a stiff climb on top of a heavy breakfast.

Once over the top and into Caithness, the final county of the walk, I kept coming across hints that I was getting close to the end. Two cyclists passed me on a tandem.

'Going to John O'Groats?' said the rider on the back.

'Trying to,' I said.

'So are we,' he said. 'Should be there by this afternoon.'

I had been meeting a lot of cyclists over this stretch of the walk. Hundreds more cyclists than walkers go End to End each year, and I was always pleased to see them. They were a cheerful bunch and would always wave. They helped to make up for not seeing many other walkers in the far north.

To pass the time, as I walked along, I started taking notice of the miscellaneous junk discarded at the side of the road and the flattened remains of assorted road kill. Most of it was pretty predictable. There were a lot of squashed rabbits, quite a few hedgehogs and a couple of weasels. Then, at the side of the road on the steep descent into Berridale, lying dead in the bracken, there was a stag, as grand as any which had graced the walls of the hotel in Helmsdale. There didn't seem to be a mark on him except for a thin trickle of blood which had seeped from one of his nostrils. I nearly gave the hotel a ring, I'm quite sure they could have found space for him on one of their walls.

The litter was less interesting: endless plastic pop bottles, flattened Irn Bru cans (Scotland is the only place where anyone drinks Irn Bru), assorted and unidentifiable mechanical bits which must have fallen off cars, the front spoiler from a Vauxhall Carlton and, just outside Ramscraigs, a bra and an empty box of Viagra tablets.

I stopped for a break, sitting on the steps of the war

226

memorial in Berridale. One of the great things about a walk like this was that I found I was noticing all sorts of local features of the country I was walking through and I'd been taking note of all the war memorials I'd passed right since Land's End. As war memorials go, the one in Berridale seemed very big and was engraved with an awful lot of names for such a small and remote community. As I progressed north substantial war memorials with long lists of the dead became a notable feature of the area. There were similarly impressive memorials at Latheron and Lyth. They may have been small communities but they sent a lot of soldiers away to the wars and an awful lot of those soldiers never came home.

There was a long stretch of pavement leading into the village of Dunbeath, which made a pleasant change from having to walk on the road. I was quite taken with the little towns and villages I passed through, like Brora, Helmsdale and Dunbeath. I came to look upon them as attractive pearls threaded on the ugly string which was the A9.

I had hoped to find somewhere for a cup of tea in Dunbeath but all I found was a Spa shop, which I was really surprised to find open because it was a Sunday afternoon. I went in and bought a Kit Kat and a carton of orange juice then sat outside on a wall and scoffed them. When I tried to move my right calf had cramped up so for the next mile and a half I was reduced to a stiff-legged hobble.

About the time my cramp freed up was the time I walked off the map. There was a little corner, just north of Dunbeath and south of Wick, which fell off the two main Landranger sheets. It was only about eight miles and I could have bought another map to cover it but it was all roadwalking and I didn't think there was much chance that I'd get lost, so I told myself that it was not worth the extra weight. If I was to be really truthful it was actually because I was just too tight-fisted to shell out for another map for such a tiny bit of roadwalking. So instead I cut a bit out of Sarah's old road atlas and navigated by that.

Tiny map-less section of roadwalking it may have been but it was an important and pivotal part of this the last leg of the walk because, just a little beyond the village of Latheron, and with great rejoicing, after it had been my constant companion for some forty-five miles, the A9 finally turned off and headed north for Thurso. But any celebrations were just a little premature: it was replaced by its bastard son, the A99.

Just a Stick and a Hotel

I stayed overnight at Lybster and next morning at Occumster, after just a short walk, I finally turned off the A roads altogether and onto a long straight single track road which would eventually lead to Watten. It felt like heaven. I timed gaps of twenty minutes and thirty-five minutes between cars.

For a mile or two there were scattered farmsteads on either side of the road and at Roster I walked off my, by now well thumbed and limp, bit of Sarah's road atlas and onto the last map of the walk, Landranger sheet twelve, Thurso and Wick (with 'John O'Groats' written in smaller letters underneath).

The owner of Camster Lodge was standing chatting over the fence to some council workers who were clearing weeds from the road.

'Are you walking to John O'Groats?' he asked as I walked past. 'Not far now.'

The country was open scrubby grassland with occasional patches of heather and some scattered conifer plantations. But these were not like the conifers of the Great Glen Way, they were not the dark beasts which seemed to hem me in. They were wild, ragged and wind blown Scots pines, which added to the impression of wildness, of being on high open ground with a big, big sky overhead.

To add a bit of interest, halfway through the day's walk I stopped at the Grey Cairns of Camster, a Neolithic burial site which consists of three large stone cairns, well restored so that it is possible to go inside two of them. It was a bit of a crawl on all fours along a low passage but inside it was surprisingly light, bright enough to take some photos. Then I crawled back down the passage again, remembering to close the little bronze gate, so the sheep didn't get in and leave their visiting cards.

I stayed at the Brown Trout in Watten. Next morning I was sitting up in bed drinking my coffee. It was to be the last day of the walk proper but it was important, or so I told myself, not to get carried away. There were still eighteen miles to cover. I had to keep reminding myself, it's just another day of the walk, just another small part of the whole.

I walked past Watten Loch then it was mostly long straight roads disappearing into the distance and crossing a seemingly endless number of low ridges. My map showed that I was walking past Stanstill Farm. Now I really could boast that I'd walked myself to a standstill.

As I walked along the ruler-straight and featureless roads I noticed a strange kind of optical illusion starting to occur. A building or a farm would appear on the horizon but would never seem to get any closer. It would just seem to hang there, no matter how hard or how fast I tried to walk towards it. And then, quite suddenly, and with no warning at all, I would be upon it and just as quickly past, and it would slowly recede into the distance again. The country up there in that far northern corner of Caithness was surprisingly flat and open. It really felt as if I was on an island. I had the sensation that the coast was closing in on me from two sides, a feeling of having walked myself into a corner.

In the far distance a mobile phone mast appeared on the horizon and went through its long and tantalising process of never seeming to get closer, then, when it suddenly appeared alongside, I crested a low ridge and there, stretched out in front of me, was the sea. The sea, glittering in the afternoon sun. I had no idea I was so close. And offshore, perhaps a mile or so away, was Stroma and the Orkney Islands.

There was still a little way to cover, past Canisbay Church where Jan de Groot, John O'Groats himself, was buried, then turn left, down a short lane and I was there, journey's end, the stick and the hotel.

Things were pretty hectic by the John O'Groats signpost. There were lots of Lycra-clad cyclists either arriving or departing. Two lads were holding their bikes up overhead while their support team were busy popping champagne corks. I was the only walker finishing that afternoon and I had to queue to have my photograph taken. Then I quickly left the signpost to its besieging cyclists and slipped away to the Journey's End Café to have a cup of tea.

The stick (the signpost) might have been in fine fettle and doing terrific business, but the John O'Groats Hotel was boarded up and in a sorry state of repair. I was especially saddened by this because all through the walk I'd been holding in my mind the picture of the start of the 1960 Billy Butlin Race, when all the competitors surged away from the start and the John O'Groats Hotel was standing proudly in the background. The photographer who took my photo by the signpost told me that there were plans well advanced to renovate and reopen the hotel soon. I do hope so.

I stayed over at John O'Groats and before I headed for home took a walk the mile or two further on to Duncansby Head. This wild headland, with its lighthouse on the very northeasterly tip of mainland Scotland with the gulls and fulmars flying past, was, for me, the true end of the walk.

It didn't matter a damn to the world in general of course, but it gave me something of a warm glow inside to think that the most significant part of those first three years since I had finished work had been spent doggedly making my way from Land's End to John O'Groats under my own steam. And it had achieved for me what I hoped it would. I was no longer an ex-worker casting around for something to do. The stressed face with its dark shadows under the eyes, which had been the norm when I was at work, had gone for good. I was busy, feeling fulfilled and fitter than I'd been for years.

As an achievement I'm proud of it but I don't think I should get carried away. I was happy for most of my life, doing a regular day job, but, when the world of work found me superfluous to requirements, with a goodly dose of luck and just a tiny bit of pigheadedness, I was able to walk the whole length of Britain and only stop when I reached John O'Groats. And, as an experience, well, I wouldn't have missed it for the world.